Praise for *Fierce Love*

"Susan Scott does a superb job of teaching couples how to create compelling conversations and foster true connection and a fierce love that will withstand the test of time and grow stronger over the years. Every couple should read this book!"

—Marshall Goldsmith, *New York Times* #1 bestselling author of *Triggers, Mojo*, and *What Got You Here Won't Get You There*

"In *Fierce Love*, Susan Scott creates a brilliant yet simple guide that inspires, and frames the most important conversations necessary to create understanding, empathy, and connection between two people. These are the tools to create deep and enduring relationships that last!"

—Gregory Dickow, senior pastor of Life Changers International Church

"Love is often expressed sentimentally and romantically. In *Fierce Love*, Susan Scott offers a pungent vision of love as a real conversation between two authentic people with no topic off the table. After identifying the myths of love, she offers a model, and a list of the conversations authentic lovers should have. Bereft of romanticism and filled with directness, this book will help any couple live their relationship in a different way. We recommend it to all couples who want to move from good to great."

—Harville Hendrix and Helen LaKelly Hunt, authors of *Getting the Love You Want: A Guide for Couples*

"In *Fierce Love*, Susan Scott candidly addresses an issue that commonly plagues many of our romantic relationships: lack of deep, vulnerable, and honest conversations. With compelling narrative and actionable steps, Scott helps readers harness the power of meaningful conversations to transform guarded love into fearless love that will unite couples for the long haul."

—Jenny Albers, author of *Courageously Expecting*

"Our relationships, our family, can and should be our biggest gift, even though I'm often tempted to treat them as my biggest pain in the butt. Susan Scott teaches us how to fight for this love—gently but fiercely—as imperfect but perfectly lovable beings."

—Anna Lind Thomas, author of *We'll Laugh About This Someday*

"In a time where many people are struggling with their relationships, we need voices that provide us with the courage, clarity, and skill to nurture our relationships and resolve recurring issues. Whether we are married or dating, we all need to have the conversations that may have eluded us. As I often say, in order for us to be great at anything, we need instruction. Susan Scott provides the necessary instruction while serving as a sisterly friend, with a great sense of humor, who helps us connect with our intimate partners at a deep level."

—Dondré Whitfield, actor and author of *Male vs. Man*

fierce
love

Also by Susan Scott

*Fierce Love: A Journal for Couples: 8 Conversations
to a Happier, Healthier Relationship*
*Fierce Leadership: A Bold Alternative to the Worst
"Best" Practices of Business Today*
*Fierce Conversations: Achieving Success at Work &
in Life, One Conversation at a Time*

Fierce Love

Creating a Love That Lasts—

One Conversation at a Time

Susan Scott, *New York Times*
Bestselling Author

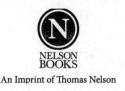

NELSON
BOOKS

An Imprint of Thomas Nelson

Fierce Love

© 2022 Susan Scott

Published in Nashville, Tennessee, by Nelson Books, an imprint of Thomas Nelson. Nelson Books and Thomas Nelson are registered trademarks of HarperCollins Christian Publishing, Inc.

"Letter of Resignation" by William Baer from *Bocage and Other Sonnets*. © Texas Review Press, 2008. Reprinted with permission.

"Summons" by Robert Francis, reprinted from *Collected Poems: 1936–1976*. Copyright © 1976 by Robert Francis. Published by the University of Massachusetts Press. Reprinted with permission.

"Hafiz" and "Covers Her Face with Both Hands" by Hafiz, reprinted from *The Gift, Poems by Hafiz, the Great Sufi Master*, renderings by Daniel Ladinsky, Penguin Books, 1999. Reprinted with permission.

Thomas Nelson titles may be purchased in bulk for educational, business, fundraising, or sales promotional use. For information, please e-mail SpecialMarkets@ThomasNelson.com.

Any internet addresses, phone numbers, or company or product information printed in this book are offered as a resource and are not intended in any way to be or to imply an endorsement by Thomas Nelson, nor does Thomas Nelson vouch for the existence, content, or services of these sites, phone numbers, companies, or products beyond the life of this book.

ISBN 978-1-4002-3326-7 (Audiobook)

Library of Congress Cataloging-in-Publication Data

Names: Scott, Susan, 1944- author.
Title: Fierce love : creating a love that lasts-one conversation at a time / Susan Scott, New York Times bestselling author.
Description: Nashville, Tennessee : Nelson Books, 2022. | Summary: "New York Times bestselling author Susan Scott guides couples through eight must-have conversations to create a fierce love that stands the test of time and grows stronger over the years"-- Provided by publisher.
Identifiers: LCCN 2021037417 (print) | LCCN 2021037418 (ebook) | ISBN 9781400233236 (hardcover) | ISBN 9781400233250 (ebook)
Subjects: LCSH: Couples. | Man-woman relationships. | Love.
Classification: LCC BF636.7.G76 S355 2022 (print) | LCC BF636.7.G76 (ebook) | DDC 646.7/7--dc23
LC record available at https://lccn.loc.gov/2021037417
LC ebook record available at https://lccn.loc.gov/2021037418

Printed in the United States of America
22 23 24 25 26   LSC   10 9 8 7 6 5 4 3 2 1

When I pick up a book, I flip to the dedication, which is always to someone else and not to me. Not this book. This one's for you if you love and are not loved, if you are loved and do not love, if you don't love and are not loved (you're breaking my heart), and if you love and are loved, which of course is the ultimate experience we all want to have. I hope this book will help you get there.

WITH YOU KNOW WHAT,
SUSAN SCOTT
SEPTEMBER 2021

It
Is all
Just a love contest
And I never
Lose.
Now you have another good reason
To spend more time
With
Me.

HAFIZ

Contents

Contents

Introduction

Love doesn't make itself, you know. We make it. Or fail to make it. And we unmake it as well. It's not like God is up there *ex machina-ing* what happens in our lives. Certainly not the amount of love we have in our lives. Or don't have.

You can't make yourself love someone, neither can you make someone love you. What you can do is behave and speak in a way that would entice love if it happened to be in the vicinity, so that love would want to hang out with you for a while. What you can do is be a loving and lovable human being.

There are so many things that scream for our attention. Work, children, money, errands. It's the rare couple who turns their attention to the conversations they are having, and yet conversations are the fulcrum that enable us to accomplish our most important goals, especially regarding the quality of our relationships.

How much love you have is up to *you* and while it may seem complicated, it isn't. Not really. It's all about our conversations. By having honest, courageous, meaningful conversations with your partner, you can foster true connection and a fierce love that will withstand the test of time and grow stronger over the years.

"I love you" doesn't quite do the trick. We've heard that so often, the effect can be blunted. No magic there and it's not a conversation. But there are magic words, important questions, and a few epiphanies along the way, like those pieces inside a kaleidoscope, and when one drops, the entire picture changes.

First, I'd like you to meet Louise and Tom.

THE END

It was a bright, cool afternoon in April when Louise Kimball threw two wedding rings into Lake Windermere, stunning her husband, Tom, who had, seconds earlier, reluctantly removed his ring and placed it in the palm of his wife's hand.

She had asked him to give it to her, had held out her hand for it, and when he had asked her why, she hadn't answered. So Tom twisted it off, a bit anxiously, and gave it to her. She coaxed her own ring off, closed her fist around both, kissed her fist. Then, as if hurling a shot in shot put, she drew back, raised her hand up and past her right ear, and with a sob, launched the rings as far as she could out over the lake. The rings' trajectory into the sweet, clean air was high and, as they flew, they parted, arched downward, and dropped into the lake. It received them with hardly any acknowledgment, closing over them with two tiny splashes that were barely visible from the shore.

When the rings left Louise's hand, Tom gasped. They were both shocked at what she had done and stood, staring. When a pair of swans, paired for life, glided serenely into view, Tom's body sagged beside her. She turned to face him and said quietly, "Now we will always remember the exact moment and place when our marriage ended."

Louise had arrived at clarity an hour earlier. She had persuaded Tom to add two days to their business meetings in London so that they could visit the Lake District in Northern England. That morning, as they walked a meandering path alongside stone fences and hedgerows choked with foxglove and Queen Anne's lace, then descended to the River Rothay and Lake Windermere, Tom had stumped gloomily and silently in front of her. *He only walks beside me when others are watching*, Louise thought.

She tried—and failed—to lift Tom's mood, to enlist him in the pleasure of being in nature—the birdsong, a gentle, fragrant breeze, the glinting lake—but it was clear he wasn't happy.

Around noon they came to a clearing, and Louise suggested they stop to eat the lunch the B&B owner had packed for them. They sat quietly until Louise said, "You don't seem to be enjoying yourself."

Tom didn't raise his eyes from the ground as he said, "Frankly, I'd rather be golfing."

That was the moment when she knew it was over. After ten years of marriage—playing at marriage—they were done. Really, truly, irretrievably finished.

"Louise" and "Tom" aren't the couple's real names, of course. But they are real people and their story is true. Louise is a real person who ended her marriage rather dramatically.

What brought her to that moment, that action? Why was Tom's response the very last straw? How had Louise traveled from "I most certainly do" to "I'm so done, I can't even tell you."

We will revisit Louise and Tom, will consider what brought them to that moment, because while most marriages don't end as dramatically as theirs, many do end. Relationships that began so well will fail, and now we're into the next phase: the divvying up of possessions, deciding who gets the dog, who gets the children on holidays.

A CHORUS LINE

In 1975 Marvin Hamlisch was hired to write the music for *A Chorus Line*. Set on the bare stage of a Broadway theater, the musical is centered on seventeen dancers auditioning for spots on a chorus line. During rehearsals, the first run-through was so bad they called it the towering inferno. Marvin said that it took him seven or eight months to figure out what the show was really about. One day during rehearsal, Michael Bennett, the choreographer, took a piece of chalk, drew a line on the floor and said, "That's the line we're all behind."

Bam! Got it. The common denominator of all those people was wanting, hoping, to cross that line. "God, I hope I get it." And the killer was the desperation. "Oh God, I need this job. I really need this job."

All of a sudden *A Chorus Line* wasn't about dancers who were showing off. It was about people who were desperate for this thing in their lives. Each character began to emerge as an individual, but there was the theme of the line on the floor, wanting to cross that line. Now people in the audience who were not dancers themselves could identify with the dancers on the stage.

What's the line we are all desperate to cross? The line some have crossed only to fail and now find themselves standing behind it again? We all want the same thing. The line we want to cross, the thing we are auditioning for, with ambitions as achingly poignant as the dancers in *A Chorus Line*, is love. We are desperate for it. *God, I hope I find it. Oh God, I need this.*

Love. One of the most-used words in the English language, the most misunderstood. *How, who, when, where?* What kind of love? How does this translate to two people, face-to-face, every day?

For two decades I have had the privilege of working within global organizations. In fact, for several years I traveled so extensively that I remember sitting down in the Sydney Opera House and reaching for my seat belt! Although the focus of my work was coaching individuals and teams on how to elevate the conversations central to their success, so often the most important thing on the hearts and minds of individuals was the quality of their relationships at home. When things were rocky there, it was hard to be focused and effective at work.

During the thousands of hours of conversations with people about their relationships, I can't say I've learned anything useful from couples who sit and beam at everyone after having declared that in their long marriages they have never fought, that it's always been wonderful between them. If you and I were sitting side by side, you might hear me mutter, "Ha, bloody ha!" because I would be thinking, *Somewhere early in your marriage, you struck an agreement to withhold what you were really thinking and feeling. You became accustomed to lying to each other, lies of omission, anything to keep the peace. Consequently, you have settled for very little.*

A bit harsh and judgmental on my part, I know, but that's what comes up for me.

I am more interested in talking with people who have weathered storms and lived to tell about it. Most people whose work I admire developed their approach out of personal devastation. I want to spend time with them. They don't tell us that they were walking down their perfect, peaceful road with nary a care and then got this idea that they want to share with us. No, most of them have been in some really tough places, had lost "it," were unhappy, were failing in the eyes of others (and usually in their own as well). Maybe there's something wrong with me, but when I hear someone say, "I've had this perfect life and I will share the secrets of my success and happiness with you," my ears clamp shut and I look for a way out of the room.

One of my favorite relationship teachers is a friend who separated from his wife and introduced me to the term THFKAH, which stands for The House Formerly Known As Home. He told me that every time he visited THFKAH, his wife handed him another black trash bag full of his stuff. When he saw some black trash bags in the back of a friend's car, he asked, "Wife throw you out?" "Yeah, how'd you know?" "Trash bags. Dead giveaway." Sad but true.

Back to you and me. When a relationship ends, we just want to walk away, get on with our lives, hoping and expecting to do better next time. But we don't do better next time. So let's figure out how my friend got from "home" to THFKAH, what brought Louise to that moment at the edge of the lake, and what might have saved their marriages.

There *are* wonderful, beautiful relationships out there, but even those have tough moments. I recently had tea with a neighbor on Orcas Island who told me that she was madly in love with her partner of seven years and that he feels the same way about her. At our annual islander gathering to make sauerkraut, she said, "Whenever I feel we are being less than we could be, we talk about it. It's not always a long conversation. Sometimes it's simply a reminder that we could settle for mediocrity or we could create something truly exceptional. Our relationship is wonderful because it's a decision we make over and over."

A few weeks after that conversation, a mutual friend told me that he had overheard quite a few yelling, screaming fights between these two. Dang! Well, nobody's perfect. Sometimes it's two steps forward, one step backward. It seems that when we describe our relationships as pretty perfect, we may be affirming what we wish it was like, when the reality is quite different. It's especially painful when one or both parties don't know how to fight fair.

Do you ever wonder how your children might describe the disagreements in your home? In *The Nix*, a hilarious and deeply touching novel about a son and the mother who left him as a child and how his search to uncover the secrets of her life leads him to reclaim his own, author Nathan Hill wrote, "Samuel thought how his father married to his mother was like a spoon married to a garbage disposal."

We all recognize that relationships, like life, rarely travel in a straight line. In fact, I have often said that life is curly. Don't try to straighten it out. There are transitions in every relationship. Torrents, pauses, windings, disappearances, cascades, successive metamorphoses. Joy ebbs and flows, subsides. Along the way, we need conversations that produce astonishment and surprise, that provide us with new nourishment.

My aim is to help you have conversations central to the success and happiness of your primary relationship. If you have opened this book, it may be because your relationship is struggling or it has ended, and you'd like to do better next time.

During hard times, particularly times that feel like a crisis, relationships accelerate, for good or not so good. I suspect that years down the road, research will discuss how relationships were affected by the COVID-19 pandemic. Enforced togetherness amplified all that was working in relationships and all that was not working, not healthy. Many couples struggled or parted because they were not able to talk through their issues in a way that enriched the relationship. They didn't know how to stop a fight in the making and transform the mood, the emotions, the words being hurled over the kitchen counter into something gentler, warmer, productive.

Maybe you're dating and want to navigate more skillfully than the last time, but each failed relationship takes a toll.

In *Redhead by the Side of the Road*, Anne Tyler wrote:

> The thing about old girlfriends, Micah reflected, is that each one subtracts something from you. You say goodbye to your first great romance and move on to the next, but you find you have less to give to the next. A little chip of you has gone missing; you're not quite so wholly *there* in the new relationship. And less there in the one after that, and even less in the one after that one.

While this can be true, it is possible to regroup, to gather up all the pieces of ourselves we may have left behind and come into a new relationship whole and healthy. Don't give up.

Perhaps you just married and want to keep your relationship happy, healthy, and headed in the right direction. Or your long-term relationship may have settled into a sleepy routine and you'd like to wake it up. Perhaps, like Oliver Twist, you want more. Not more porridge. You want more passion, more connection, more fun, more peace, more [fill in the blank]. And you sense in your bones that there is more to be enjoyed, if only you knew how to find it.

Complicating the matter is the fact that there are two people in a relationship, so how might you entice someone else to step up to the plate with you? Perhaps when you've tried to talk about this with your partner, the conversations have failed to produce the results you want.

Recently, I received an email from someone who was reading my first book, *Fierce Conversations*. I responded with a few suggestions and he wrote back:

> Wanting to give something back, I offer you this:
> The book is going slowly.
> After the kids are in bed, there is some time
> to sit together in the living room and read.
> She likes on the couch. I prefer the chair that faces her.
> I read a page and glance up.

> When our eyes meet my ears hear all the whispers
> of what was not said today.
> No contest.

I had to sit and breathe for a few minutes, unsure whether he was saying they were able to connect with a glance or that they didn't say what they should have said. Somehow, it didn't matter. There was awareness and that was enough.

This book is focused on the conversations central to the success of two people in real time when things are good and not so good. It's for people who love each other but don't know *how* to love each other or aren't very good at it. Or who used to love each other and want to get it back. Or who are thinking about loving each other, trying to love each other. Or whose relationships keep crashing and they wonder why. And it's for those who want to enrich an already healthy relationship. It is about our face-to-face, everyday, up-close-and-personal attempts to give and receive love.

We'll try to make sense of why our efforts are successful, when they are, and why they fail miserably, when they do. What conversations are essential for any two people who love each other or want to love each other? And how do you have them? You'll also learn how to "Defend Against the Dark Arts" that attempt to cripple or destroy relationships.

By the way, you and your partner will disagree sometimes. You just need to do it better.

This book is aimed at helping you and your current or future partner navigate beyond the accepted platitudes about love and replace long-accepted notions guaranteed to get you in trouble with insights that make far more sense. We're going to get real. We're going to put our cards on the table.

We will come to understand how important our conversations with our partners are, that each conversation can be a small diminishment. String them together over months, years, a lifetime, and it's as if we pulled off

our own wings. As Rumi wrote in his poem "A Night Full of Talking":
"You have to do some hard things for that swan to spread her wings, those
beautiful wings."

We will answer questions.

- How can we get our wings back?
- How can we wake things up when we are no longer lovers, just
  housemates?
- Why does it take so little to send love running out the door?
- Why do we leave so much out when we "tell the truth"?
- Why are our conversations so careful?
- Why can't/don't we say what we're really thinking and feeling?
- What is the conversation that we've been unable to have that, if we
  could have it, might change everything?

I've had robust conversations with friends about these questions, and
we've also discussed the three most common experiences of love.

1. I love and am not loved.
2. I am loved and do not love.
3. I love and am loved. Fully, completely, no question.

This book offers a path to the third experience.

I want you to learn how to create love. Every day. On purpose. Create
more and more of it. Fill your home with it until you and your partner breathe
it in and out like oxygen. If you have children, they are watching, listening.
How you and your partner talk with each other, how you express affection and
respect for each other, is the model they will attempt to duplicate when they
look for love. I want your example to be stellar. Don't settle for less.

HOW THIS BOOK IS ORGANIZED

Part 1 clarifies the role of conversations in a relationship and serves as the
foundation for fierce love. It also defines the difference between love and

fierce love and how you can gauge the health of *your* relationship. Part 2 addresses the five myths that mislead and derail relationships. Part 3 offers a primer on the seven principles of fierce conversations and a detailed road map to eight conversations that will create a rich and satisfying bond with your partner.

Throughout this book you will find passages from literature that illustrate what I wanted to say better than I could say it. Importantly, as you read this book, imagine that you and I are together. Perhaps we are having a cup of coffee or tea, a glass of wine or a beer. And we are talking. That is how I'm writing to you, as if you and I are sitting together and having a conversation. I am not writing to a vast audience. I am writing and speaking to *you*, the person who is reading this book right now.

When asked why it took so long for me to write the book that has been circling me for years, I quote Ernest Hemingway: "The great thing is to last and get your work done and see and hear and learn and understand; and write when there is something that you know; and not before; and not too damned much after."

I have figured out some things that I believe will help you, although what I write is not nearly as important as what *you* think and feel as you read this book. Your thoughts, your current situation, the issues you're dealing with today, your hopes for the future, and how the conversations in this book can be of help to you. And your emotions. We humans make decisions first for emotional reasons, second for rational reasons. Our emotions give the lit match something to ignite, so don't push your emotions away. They are talking to you. Pay attention.

Also, this book is for your personal use, a user's manual, so grab a pen and mark it up, write in it, underline, or grab a piece of paper or personal journal to jot down your thoughts. There is also a companion piece, *Fierce Love: A Journal for Couples*, available that complements this book and encourages you to really interact with the conversations and questions. I'm also preparing an online course that will help you on your journey. If you do the work, you will uncover some profound truths and create a plan to enrich your love life.

A brief word about language in this book. I struggled with what to call the person you love or want to love. In *Game of Thrones*, Drogo calls

Daenerys "Moon of My Life." She calls him "My Sun and Stars." It would get a bit tedious to talk like this all the time. "How long are you going to be in the bathroom, Moon of My Life?" "As long as it takes, My Sun and Stars. Use the one in the basement."

Millennials like "Babe," as in "Hey, Babe, let's . . ." Brits like "Darling," as in "Of course, Darling, whatever you say . . ." often said through clenched teeth. I've settled on "partner" and sometimes I will say "he" and at other times "she."

It would be easy to feel overwhelmed with the notion of fierce love and to think of this quest as too demanding and too time-consuming in your already busy days. You might easily feel that there are just too many conversations between your current reality and what you desire. You might wonder if it is possible to truly feel at home in your relationship. I hope to reassure you that it is, and although the stakes are high, the steps are small.

It is important to start slowly, to cull through the myths around romantic love and find inroads to a more realistic view of love and a more fulfilling way to engage with our partners.

It is important that you practice the conversations. None of us were born with the courage to confront ourselves and our relationships with fullness and honesty. Bravery is a muscle that can be developed. The experience of enduring love, fierce love, is simply a continuing practice of showing up authentically. We'll take it one conversation at a time.

When is the right time for these conversations? Now is the right time.

PART 1

The Idea of Fierce Love

The only thing that matters is love.

Yeah, but what does that *mean*?

Have you noticed that most of the lyrics in love songs aren't helpful when it comes to you and me, nose to nose, eye to eye, every day, especially when the blush has gone off the rose?

Jim, a friend of mine, admitted,

I had a long line of failed relationships. I'd been married twice and was engaged in a long string of serial monogamous failures. One of the more kind titles for my relationship history was "infatuation vampire." I kept up a well-practiced emotional barricade, showing enough of me to give the illusion of connection, but nothing past that.

After a particularly dismal personal relationship failure, I decided to take stock of my relationship past and take a look at my present relationship forecast. The forecast looked bleak and familiar: excited at the beginning, bored in the middle (sometimes after a day or two), and a mixture of relief and depression in the end. It was time—over time—for a change. I decided I truly wanted a healthy relationship. My problem was I had no idea how to do that. I remember going to a group of my friends and saying, "I just realized that I have no idea how to make a relationship work." Their accumulated response could be easily stated in one word: "Duh!"

Funny and true. Who wouldn't appreciate maintenance-free, guaranteed-fresh, organic, and self-cleaning relationships? We want the happily ever after of fairy tales and the conflict-free marriages that only exist in televised fantasies. Real relationships take time, energy, and daily care and feeding.

The first shift in the creation of a fierce relationship is to treat it as if it's alive and breathing. In fact, dogs and relationships are very similar. For instance, what would happen if you stopped feeding your dog—or any pet for that matter? I can think of many outcomes, none of them pretty. Some potential outcomes are:

- If the lack of food went on for a while, he'd die.
- He might go to the neighbors looking for something to nourish him.
- He'd get tricky and try to get or sneak food in other ways.
- He would get by on crumbs and live in resentment.
- If he's submissive he'll start to beg.
- If he's dominant he'll get mad and bite you.

For a relationship to be healthy, you need to feed it healthy food—daily. We discredit truly healthy relationships by saying, "They are so lucky." We give more credit to pet owners for their healthy pets than we give to couples for the care and feeding they give to nurture their relationships.

> It turns out that *what* we talk about and *how* we talk about it determine whether our relationships will thrive, flatline, or fail.

As you move forward in this book, I will give you feeding tips for your relationship—the conversations that will nourish it. These will require time and attention. It is no different than wanting to become a talented painter but having no time to invest in learning the skills. You could look up the odds of succeeding in the dictionary under "fat chance." Neglect and underfeeding give you a relationship that is skinny, filled with resentment, and barely alive. It seems that the choice would be easy, but cultural relationship myths like "If I find the right one it won't take any effort" take a long time to die.

It turns out that *what* we talk about and *how* we talk about it determine whether our relationships will thrive, flatline, or fail.

1

The Conversation *Is* the Relationship

With thee conversing I forget all time.
—JOHN MILTON

Years ago, I heard Yorkshire-born poet and author David Whyte speak at a conference. David spoke of the newly married young man who is often frustrated, even a little irritated, that his lovely spouse, to whom he has pledged his troth and with whom he hopes to spend the rest of his life, wants to talk—yet again—about the same thing they just talked about last night, last weekend. The topic? The quality of their relationship.

He wonders, *Why are we talking about this again? I thought we settled this. Could we just have one huge conversation about our relationship and then coast for a year or two?* Apparently not, because here she is again.

Eventually, if he's been paying attention, it dawns on him. "This robust, ongoing conversation I have been having with my wife is not about the relationship. The conversation *is* the relationship."

This was the first idea that transformed how I think about relationships. The idea was simple, even obvious, but I had managed to miss the formula.

Conversation = Relationship

When I heard David, I had just left my marriage and was deeply sad. My husband and I had found a hundred wrong ways to resolve our issues, and since none of them worked, we had given up. Our home had fallen silent. For me, this idea that the conversation *is* the relationship was a genuine, card-carrying epiphany that explained everything. It moved into my head and heart, pitched a tent, and built a campfire. It wasn't leaving. Ever.

If you recognize that there may be something to this idea that the conversation *is* the relationship, then if the conversation stops, well, you can do the math. Or if you and your partner add another topic to the list of things you can't talk about because it would wreck another weekend, all the possibilities for the relationship grow smaller and all the possibilities for the individuals in the relationship grow smaller, until one day you realize that you are making yourself quite small in every conversation, behaving as if you are just the space around your shoes, engaged in yet another conversation so empty of meaning it crackles.

When our conversations become constrained, when we avoid topics that might cause upset, when we accept behavior or comments that are hurtful, we are no longer aiming for harmony but rather a sort of deafness that allows us to stay in a relationship longer than we should. Our senses become dulled and we end up settling, even when we are anguished.

Here's the good news: while no single conversation is guaranteed to change the trajectory of a relationship, any single conversation can.

Not just any conversation. Our usual ones aren't conversations at all. The word *conversation* comes from the Latin *conversari*, which means to associate with, an exchange of ideas and sentiments. It begins with *con*, which is Spanish for "with." Sadly, many people don't have conversations. They have versations. There is no talking *with*. There is only talking *to*.

> While no single conversation is guaranteed to change the trajectory of a relationship, any single conversation can.

In addition to talking *with* versus *to* your partner, a conversation capable of changing the trajectory of your relationship must be fierce. So before going any further, let's clarify what this means.

What is a fierce conversation?

The simplest definition is one in which we come out from behind ourselves into the conversation and make it real by disclosing what we really think and feel. Many people are in relationships where they don't feel seen or understood. It would be a mistake to blame this on someone else. If we wish to be seen, we have to show up. We have to be real. Given this definition, I'm always puzzled when people demur, "You're not suggesting that all our conversations have to be fierce, are you?"

Well, since, at its most fundamental, fierce conversations are about being *real*, then yes, I'd like all of my conversations to be fierce. While many people fear being real, it's the unreal conversations that should scare us to death, because they are incredibly expensive.

It's a conscious choice to show up truthfully, to be current with everyone in your life, to travel light, agenda-free. Wonderful things can happen in a room when two people tell the truth.

And still the long face.

I ask, "What are you thinking?"

A long pause, a deep sigh, then, "I don't know. I don't think that would work with my husband. There are things we don't bring up because they'd only stir up problems."

This makes me speculate about the person's daily struggle, what it must be like to remain hidden as a way of life. I wonder what the perceived rules are at home and how this person's partner would describe their relationship.

> While many people fear being real, it's the unreal conversations that should scare us to death, because they are incredibly expensive.

In *The Nightingale*, Kristin Hannah wrote: "I always thought it was what I wanted . . . to be loved and admired. Now I think perhaps I'd like to be known." No chance of that if we fail to show up authentically.

Being real doesn't mean that you must disclose every thought you've ever had or everything you've ever done. There are chapters in every life that do not need to be read aloud. Fierce conversations do, however, require emotional honesty. For example, telling someone how you are feeling in the moment or sharing that something your partner said or did hurt you, angered you, or warmed your heart, making you feel even closer to your partner.

You may be asking yourself, "How real should I be? Doesn't that require some tiptoeing so as not to upset my partner? Shouldn't I be careful about what I say?"

Nope. A careful conversation is a failed conversation because it simply postpones the conversation that wants and needs to take place.

In fact, the fear of hurting someone is most often an excuse for our cowardice, so no more dancing around the issue. You're going straight in. But you will do it in such a way that, no matter the topic, the conversation will enrich your relationship.

It would be great if we could answer the question, "Aren't most people pretty real during a conversation?" with a resounding "Yes!" But even when we are committed to authenticity, it can be surprisingly difficult.

Have you ever walked into a home and sensed that it has been staged to impress, leaving you wondering who really lives there? It's unlikely that you will meet an authentic person. Having gone to all this trouble, why demolish their carefully crafted image with reality?

We tend to project images we imagine others desire. In fact, you may have been focused on what other people think of you for so long that you have developed amnesia about who you really were when you were young and all the possibilities seemed so vast. You left that self on the curb years ago, just before a date, during which the person you displayed to a potential lover was no one you knew.

> A careful conversation is a failed conversation because it simply postpones the conversation that wants and needs to take place.

It's important to understand that authenticity is not something you have. It's something you choose.

Our true selves aren't necessarily bestowed at birth. There is no "self" out there waiting for us. We have to create who we want to be, discovering our true selves over time. And along the way we decide how much or how little of our true selves we will disclose to others.

The singer James Taylor has said, "I am myself for a living." I love that. When our lives become consistent with who we really are, rather than who we are with, others recognize it and respond.

Once you come out from behind yourself into your conversations and make them real, you will find yourself abandoning the "unreal" for the juice and motivation of clarity. You will nurture the emergence of healthier, more effective qualities and behaviors. As a result, you will move toward what you desire—a happier relationship, personal freedom, a life that simply fits you better (a lot better), and the experience of being awake, alive, and free.

2

Gradually Then Suddenly

Your dreaming self seeks to tell you something your waking ears
will not hear.
—JACQUELINE CAREY, *KUSHIEL'S CHOSEN*

The second idea that transformed the way I think about conversations and relationships arrived courtesy of Ernest Hemingway. In *The Sun Also Rises*, a character is asked how he went bankrupt. He responds, "Gradually and then suddenly." At the time I read this, I had had more than ten thousand hours of conversations with industry leaders worldwide. I thought back over important events in the personal and professional lives of my clients.

When their businesses were struggling, sometimes the questions were, How did we manage to lose our biggest customer? My most valued employee? The cohesiveness of the team?

And sometimes a distraught human being was asking, "How did I manage to lose an eighteen-year marriage that I was not prepared to lose? How is it that I find myself in a relationship from which I've absented my body and spirit? How did I lose my way? How did I get *here*?"

Once they reflected on the path that led them to a disappointing or difficult point in time professionally or personally, they remembered—often in vivid detail—the conversations that set things in motion, ensuring that they would end up exactly where they found themselves. They lost that customer, that employee, the cohesiveness of their team, their marriage, their joy one failed or one missing conversation at a time.

In fact, it was often the missing conversations for which they were paying the greatest price: the conversations they avoided for days, weeks, months, even years, caused the most devastation. This is painfully clear in many personal relationships.

In her fifth novel, *The Summer of the Bear*, journalist Bella Pollen said:

> At first, the difference in their relationship was so subtle, she barely noticed it. It was as though each sentence had one word less and each conversation was short of one sentence. Slowly but surely though, whole paragraphs began to disappear from their lives until information was being exchanged on a need-to-know basis only. It was bewildering how lonely it made her feel.

I've seen this happen. You probably have too. It begins with resignation, then slips into silence and hardens into a bitter, blaming estrangement. Sometimes there are clues. Heavy-handed hints of a slow, steady, secretive withdrawal from a marriage. Elizabeth Berg's novel *Open House* begins with this paragraph: "You know before you know, of course. You are bending over the dryer, pulling out the still-warm sheets, and the knowledge walks up your backbone. You stare at the man you love and you are staring at nothing: he is gone before he is gone."

By the same token, how did we arrive at our current happy state of affairs in the areas that matter most to us? Whenever I ask someone how he or she achieved something celebratory at work or at home, they often describe the conversations that had led to success, to happiness.

The idea I want you to embrace is that our relationships thrive, flatline, or fail gradually and then suddenly—one conversation at a time.

We all wake up when a negative "suddenly" arrives at our door.

Our relationships thrive, flatline, or fail gradually and then suddenly—one conversation at a time.

- I love you, but I don't love our life together.
- I love you, but much of what I've told you about myself is untrue.
- I love you more than I've ever loved anyone, except for someone I met at work.
- I love you, but I don't believe that you love me.
- We have fallen into a routine that is unhealthy and boring. I've been thinking of leaving.

If "suddenlys" like these are a surprise, then we've been asleep at the wheel. Perhaps we were snoozing in the passenger seat while our partner was heading in a direction we hadn't planned on.

REVISITING LOUISE

Louise's "suddenly" was the comment her husband, Tom, made on their walk around Lake Windermere. There had been hundreds of "graduallys." They had stopped telling each other how they were feeling or what was bothering them or what they wanted and needed from each other because they were terrible at it. They knew that one or both of them would quickly get triggered, language would turn blue, someone would storm out of the room, and it would get very quiet. For a long time. So they stopped even trying to talk about anything sensitive. Sex, that passionate experience of intimacy and connection? Forget it.

Louise's initial attraction to Tom had been his stunning good looks. Once they married, the main thing that kept them together was the work they shared. They were an effective and sought-after team.

Other than their work, they had different priorities and no shared interests. He gave her golf gloves. She bought him theater tickets. She didn't golf and he didn't enjoy the theater, which brings us to Louise's "suddenly."

Most people wouldn't think that a comment like "I'd rather be golfing" would end a marriage, but that was the moment Louise arrived at her "suddenly." Tom hadn't seen it coming and was shocked and confused. He had just been behaving as his usual self. There was no bad guy here. In fact, Tom was a good person. But Louise could no longer deny that she and Tom wanted very different lives in every area that mattered to both of them, and neither would ever be happy unless the other became an entirely different person, which was in no danger of happening. Most painful was the silence in which they tried to coexist. The lack of conversation. The illusion of a happy marriage. One leaving the house when the other arrived. Physical intimacy had not been part of their marriage for years. She had thought of leaving more than once, but the dream of what could be possible for them, what should be possible for them, kept her in the marriage.

She didn't know her "suddenly" would arrive as they walked along the river in the Lake District. She just knew she was miserable and that something had to change. How badly did Louise want something different for herself? Badly. Enough to end her marriage and start fresh, alone or with someone else down the road. No matter. She would no longer hang out in hope and that's why, when they stood beside Lake Windermere, she took off her wedding ring. You know the rest.

If we are shocked when we arrive at a painful "suddenly," it is because we haven't been paying attention during "gradually," and this is a problem because "gradually" is where we live most of our lives. We hadn't noticed which direction the relationship was headed. Or we pretended not to. Or we absolutely did notice but didn't know how to fix the problems. We found ourselves wondering but not saying, *Are you still in there somewhere? When I look at you sitting only a few feet away, it seems you're actually many miles away.*

In "A Ritual to Read to Each Other," poet laureate William Stafford wrote, "It is important that awake people be awake." Everyone wakes up at "suddenly." I want you to remain awake during "gradually," alert and responsive to clues—the wind has shifted and the animals are acting funny—that you're headed toward a negative "suddenly." Unlike the movies, in which bloodstains are easily detectable, the clues that the current reality is changing are often subtle, less dramatic, yet it's important that you notice them because you can almost always intervene during "gradually." The clean-up crew has to deal with "suddenly."

> Remain awake during "gradually."

Think about where you are today, your "here." What words or phrases describe your most important relationship right now or a relationship that ended?

Now imagine the relationship you desire. What words or phrases describe that relationship?

If you ask yourself, *How will I get from where I am today to where I want to be?* the answer is simple. You'll get *there* the same way you got *here*. Gradually then suddenly, one conversation at a time. Think about "one conversation at a time." If you've ever opened a combination lock on a safe, you know that one click doesn't do the job. It's only when that final click occurs that the safe opens. A conversation with someone you love is like that. It's not about trying to say something original or interesting. It's about being willing to put yourself on the edge of a conversation and seeing what happens, where it wants to go. It's about really asking, really listening. One true statement, one sincere question at a time, and you're into deep blue water. No fences, no clear destination. You may be surprised at what you hear yourself saying.

It might not require as many conversations as you imagine.

3

All Conversations
Are with Myself

Most misunderstandings in the world could be avoided if people
would simply take the time to ask, "What else could this mean?"
—SHANNON L. ALDER

How often have you left a conversation with someone and
discovered later that, apparently, the two of you participated in the same
different conversation? What you said and what she heard, or vice versa,
wasn't even on the same planet! Or someone attached a meaning and intent
to your words that never crossed your mind. This happens so often. The
experience of being understood versus misinterpreted is so compelling you
could charge admission.

Spending time with those who misinterpret us in almost every conversation causes relationships to stall or end. It's irritating, but what about *our*
possible misinterpretations? What stories are we telling ourselves during
our conversations?

Each of us experiences life through our unique context—that filter consisting of our opinions, beliefs, and attitudes—which has been shaped and
reinforced over a lifetime.

> The experience of being understood versus misinterpreted is so compelling you could charge admission.

When I think about what we've all gone through in the last few years—the refusal of some to get the COVID-19 vaccine for fear that the government was injecting a tracking device, the heartbreaking murders of George Floyd and other people of color, violence, hatred, distrust—it is clear that some beliefs are destructive, like the tree a car runs into. The tree doesn't do anything. It just stands there, unmovable. Relationships unquestionably suffer because we are not willing to let go of beliefs that, like the tree, do not serve us.

Remember when Toto pulls the curtain back in *The Wizard of Oz*, exposing the little man at the controls of the microphone and projector? Oz, the great and powerful, was orchestrating some spectacular special effects while remaining concealed. Well, we've all got our own wizard behind the curtain pulling the gears and turning the dials in our heads. Although we usually "pay no attention to the man behind the curtain," he is a chatty, wily character, both insecure and arrogant: he wants reassurance that he is right, and at the same time he is convinced he knows the capital-T truth. And he is running the show.

As Oliver Wendell Holmes wrote, "We are all tattooed in our cradles with the beliefs of our tribe; the record may seem superficial, but it is indelible." Since that man behind the curtain may not always have your best interests in mind, don't buy into his drama and don't believe everything you think.

Everything in our lives—people, places, events—has shaped who we are, what we do, and what we create. Some have no serious consequences and some are tragic. For example:

- Don't wear white after Labor Day.
- Vaccines are harmful and should be avoided.
- Climate change is not happening.
- Some ethnic groups are more valuable than others.
- I am a failure, irredeemably flawed, unlovable, bad, stupid, worthless, weak, boring, unwanted, invisible, helpless, ugly, uninteresting.

We would be quite different if we were brought up by different parents, taught by different teachers, had different friends, attended different churches or no church at all, lived on a mountaintop or in a bustling city.

The question isn't whether your beliefs or your partner's beliefs are right or wrong. The question is, Are your beliefs working for you? What results are your beliefs producing? Are your beliefs causing you to assign inaccurate or undeserved meaning to your partner's words and actions?

What's crucial to understand is that our context determines how we experience the content in our lives, including our relationships. Quite simply, our context is running our lives because it influences our behavior, and our behavior produces our results. I believe X, which causes me to behave Y, which produces results Z.

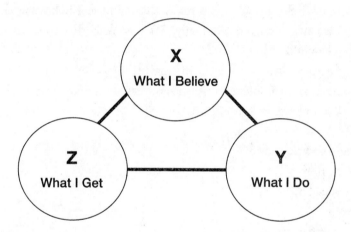

It seems we've all got baggage. It's contained in a suitcase called context, and we can't just drop it at the curb and walk away because, for most of us, our beliefs become our truths, whether they help or hinder us.

Let's apply this to your relationship, whether you are married or dating. Do you view your relationship as something to be endured for the sake of the kids or because you don't want to be alone or because you don't think you could do better? Or do you view your relationship, even with its imperfections, as a worthwhile work in progress? How would your view influence how you interact with your partner, what you do, what you say? What results would those interactions produce?

Let's say you believe that disclosing your real thoughts and feelings to your partner is risky. If that's what you believe, when your partner asks you what you're thinking, you'll duck and dodge, give the answer you think he or she wants to hear, or claim not to be thinking about anything, which is impossible unless you are a thirteen-year-old boy. If your partner asks, "What's wrong?" you'll say, "Nothing." If your partner asks, "You mad about something?" you'll say no and change the subject.

Where does that leave you? Nowhere different than you were before, and you certainly haven't enriched your relationship. In fact, the little lie between you causes unease. Something is wrong. Something is bothering you. You both know it. And you arrived at this uncomfortable state of affairs because you believe it's too risky to tell the truth. On the other hand, if you believe that disclosing what you really think and feel helps you and your partner stay awake during "gradually," it's less likely that you will arrive at a negative "suddenly."

Our context is at work even in small things. For example, while my daughter was at my home recently, she got very short texts from her husband in response to hers.

How's your day going?
K.
Are you at home?
Yes.
Can't wait to see you later.
Yep.

If my daughter believed that her husband was disengaged from the relationship and didn't care whether she was home or away, she could have read bluntness and rudeness in his replies and might have headed home hurt and angry. Thankfully, she knows her marriage is solid and sent one more text.

Pretty cryptic responses.
Sorry, cooking. Fingers sticky.

The idea that I want you to take from this is that our beliefs are running our relationships and we behave in ways guaranteed to reinforce those beliefs. Numerous beliefs are valid. The question is, Which ones will lead to the results you desire? Which filter will propel you to act in helpful, loving ways?

To make this come alive for *you*, look at the chart below and check the beliefs you hold. Don't check what you think you ought to check. Check the beliefs that you *really* hold. There will probably be checks in both columns.

I BELIEVE . . .

☐ Disclosing my real thoughts and feelings is risky.	☐ Disclosing what I really think and feel frees up energy and expands possibilities.
☐ My partner can't handle the truth, so it's better not to say anything.	☐ Though I have trouble handling the truth sometimes, I'll keep telling it and inviting it from my partner.
☐ It's important that I convince my partner that my point of view is correct.	☐ Exploring my partner's point of view will lead to better decisions for both of us.
☐ I will gain approval and affection by exchanging my authentic self for the image I imagine my partner desires.	☐ My authentic self will be expanded as my partner gets to know and love the real me.
☐ Reality can't be changed. There's no point in fighting it.	☐ Perhaps we can change reality with thoughtful conversations.
☐ The best way to support my partner is to give advice.	☐ The best way to support my partner is to ask questions that help him/her gain insight into what needs to happen.
☐ I'll keep my mouth shut. My partner probably knows best.	☐ My point of view is as valid as my partner's.
☐ I need to ignore what I'm feeling in my gut; just put my head down and pretend everything is okay.	☐ I know what I know, and what I know, I need to act on.

If you scan the list of beliefs and ask yourself how people holding those beliefs will behave, you will recognize the beliefs that enrich relationships and those that may lead to their demise. Recognizing how your beliefs affect your behavior toward your partner is worthy of contemplation.

- How often are you putting a negative spin on your partner's words that doesn't belong there?
- How often are you ascribing a motive to your partner's behavior that could be completely wrong?
- How adept are you at proving yourself right, even though your so-called truth may be causing pain?
- Do you care more about being right than being a loving partner and doing what it takes to create an extraordinary relationship?

Sometimes being "right" feels wrong, based on results. Think about this. If you are committed to always being right, you might be ignoring that little voice that is asking, "If you *are* right about this, what are the implications? What results are you getting?" If you believe, for example, that your partner can't handle the truth (which doesn't say much for your partner), then you will withhold it. And this will inevitably escalate any problems in your relationship. Gradually, gradually, off the cliff we go.

There was a time when I'd get feedback that, although my message was useful, my delivery could use some work, that I sometimes came across as harsh. My belief—which I felt was right—was, "If I'm too strong for some people, that's their problem." The result of this belief? Sometimes the way I said things, my tone, the heat with which I delivered a message, was hurtful. Who would want to spend time with someone who might wound them? It took me awhile to notice that the constant in all of my failed conversations was me. The problem wasn't that others were weak. I was the problem.

One of the beliefs that most damages our relationships is the arrogant conviction that someone in our lives isn't smart, isn't capable, isn't worthy, isn't lovable, isn't [fill in the blank]—and/or that this person is almost always wrong. Being right about a belief like this would greatly harm that relationship. If it doesn't feel wrong, it should.

Take a moment to interrogate the wizard behind your curtain, the one running your life. Write down two beliefs you currently hold about yourself or your partner that could be damaging your relationship, how you behave as a result of those beliefs, and the results they produce in your relationship. For example, "I don't dare bring up my concerns about how much my partner is drinking/our lack of intimacy/our conflicting priorities/how much we owe on our credit cards because it would just start a fight."

Would *you* like to be on the receiving end of you?

Considering how you behave toward your partner because of your beliefs, would *you* like to be on the receiving end of you?

If you recognize that a belief you hold isn't working all that well, don't cling to it as the undeniable truth. Instead, share and explore your belief with your partner.

Now that we've covered why conversations are at the center of your relationship, let's define fierce love.

4

Crossing the Bold Line

If love disappeared when we touched the fault-lines, it wouldn't
be worth much, would it?

— CLAIRE CROSS

I believe that most people want to experience the kind of romantic interactions we see in just about every movie, TV show, novel, and popular song. It's called the "love interest" and it must be worked into every plot, no matter how silly or tortured. It is the most popularized of all relationships.

Why? Because romantic love is a primary cultural myth of our time. As George Lucas explained to Steven Spielberg (these are the two who somehow squeezed a love interest into all those Indiana Jones movies), "If the boy and girl walk off into the sunset hand-in-hand in the last scene, it adds ten million to the box office."

The problem with romantic love is that it buys into the feeling of "you are the only one for me" and "if you don't love me, I'll be miserable." I remember a song with the lyrics, "I can't live if living is without you." When referring to that ballad, Paul McCartney once called it "the killer song of all time." I agreed with him until I thought about the message the song was sending. Mix a belief like this with sexual desire and we have intense focus on a love object!

Margaret Anderson is the founder and editor of the *Little Review* magazine, in which she introduced works by many of the best-known American and British writers of the twentieth century. She explained it this way: "In real love you want the other person's good. In romantic love you want the other person."

The illusion of falling in love can blind you to the suitability of a partner for a venture as delicate, intricate, and important as getting married and raising children or getting married and raising orchids.

Maurice Chevalier, a "debonair French musical-comedy star and entertainer who was known for witty and sophisticated films," observed, "Many a man has fallen in love with a girl in light so dim he would not have chosen a suit by it." Many a person has chosen a mate in light of reason dimmer than that. This blindness, as much as anything else, accounts for the many failures in the pursuit of a successful marriage.

Let's take a different path.

Fierce love speaks to the energy that flows through a relationship. Energy keeps a relationship vital. *Fierce* denotes a powerful energetic force that is present during our conversations, during lovemaking, even during a relaxing game of cards. We see our relationship as a living, breathing being, a being with a pulse, needs, and a purpose. Your job is to keep this being fed, energized, and vitally alive.

Fierce relationships are rare. When we hit the challenge of creating one, most of us settle for a careful relationship. *Careful* suppresses energy. The moment we attempt to put the careful into fierce, we start to drain it energetically. We settle into a routine. We understand the unspoken rules about which topics are and aren't okay to discuss. Nothing new here. Boring.

Think about a relationship filled with careful passion, careful conversations, careful lovemaking, careful commitment, careful satisfaction. A careful couple pretends that everything is fine until they explode in fits of victimizing and blaming fueled by their underground storage of unresolved conflicts, resentments, and avoided concerns that finally hit the light of day. Careful couples are concerned with how they look from the outside and hide anything that may displease or alarm others. They lead their lives embracing a mantra of "What might others think?"

Now think about a relationship that is fiercely passionate, filled with fierce conversations, fiercely loving, fiercely committed, and fiercely satisfying. We long for fierce relationships. The problem is we want a perpetually comfortable fierce relationship. That's like wanting guaranteed risk.

Fierce love is powerful, strong, robust, intense, uncurbed, passionate, and untamed. When a fierce couple hits challenges and obstacles in life, they bond together in strength to stand up to the challenge. Fierce couples are more concerned with the inside of the relationship, what is really going on. Consequently, they both come out from behind themselves into their relationship and make it real. The result is a relationship in which they feel safe to be the unique persons they are, safe to take a stand for what each believes in and desires.

> In a fierce relationship you face your fears. In a careful relationship you hide from them.

The thing that keeps us from daring to be authentic and thus producing a fierce relationship is fear, which has been around forever. We run into problems when we allow fear to make our decisions. When fear is in charge it takes the joy out of life. We end up staying away from what we don't want instead of moving toward what we do want.

In a fierce relationship you face your fears. In a careful relationship you hide from them, hope they go away, and search frantically for something to distract you. Hiding from fear is not new. We've been doing it as long as our species has existed. Let's work on removing it, which requires that we understand the most important thing about fierce love.

WHAT IS FIERCE LOVE?

There is a bold, compelling line between love and *fierce* love. You will begin to cross the line, dropping into a different kind of intimacy, a different way of being, a different quality of relationship once you understand and act on the central premise at the heart of fierce love:

> If you want to become a great partner, you must gain the capacity, the commitment, and the courage to connect with your partner at a deep level . . . or lower your aim.

Do you want to be a nice partner, a pretty good partner, or a great partner? If you want the latter, don't settle for conversations in which what rises to the surface is just more surface. If you do, your relationship will languish. Is that what you want? Same old, same old?

When I speak about connecting at a deep level, I think some people envision the hazard involved in putting a wet hand on the anode while the other reaches for the cathode. In truth, it's the lack of connection that is painful and can deliver two people who want to love each other to a shocking "suddenly."

It's the deep level that makes the difference. Consider water-skiing versus scuba diving. I grew up water-skiing on a lake at my grandparents' home in Chattanooga, Tennessee. As an adult, I love scuba diving in Hawaii. Water-skiing is loads of fun and you can get a tan, but when you put on a tank and go beneath the surface of the water, you are in an utterly different, beautiful world.

So while it's easy to think you know everything there is to know about your partner, there is more to discover, a deeper connection to be experienced if you are willing to venture out into those deep blue waters. And you probably had that experience once upon a time.

Let me explain.

BEGIN AGAIN FOR THE FIRST TIME

Falling in love. Ah, I remember it well. Most of us have had that experience—of literally falling into love. We fell into our lover's arms. We melted, we blended, we leaned. We talked for hours, entwined, learning, listening, disclosing. We were attentive to any change in facial expression or tone of voice, sometimes prompting, "What are you thinking?" We wanted to know as much as possible about the person with whom we were falling in love.

The trouble is, over time, the fall can become an ongoing downward trajectory in part because once a commitment is made, those conversations tend to fade and are replaced by simple exchanges. The kids, the job, what needs doing around the house. Our questions and our responses are automatic, our conversations less frequent. We coast along on the surface of the relationship because we think we know our partner and now all we need to do is learn to coexist, raise our children, feed the cat. The information we exchange—that it's supposed to be really cold next week, that the garage needs sorting—lacks warmth or humanity. It lacks intimacy.

Familiarity can breed, if not contempt, indifference, boredom. In *The Husband's Secret* by Liane Moriarty, Rachel's husband, Will, leaves her briefly for another woman, then asks to return. While they were apart, she rekindled a passionate affair with Connor, a former lover. Now that her husband is back, she wonders if she should stay with him for the sake of their young son or return to Connor. Her husband had wronged her and she had wronged him. Had they both been insane?

> They could fall in love with fresh new people or they could have the courage and humility to tear off some essential layer of themselves and reveal to each other a whole new level of otherness. A level far beyond what sort of music they liked. It seemed to her everyone had too much self-protective pride to truly strip off down to their souls in front of their long-term partners. It was easier to pretend there was nothing more to know, to fall into an easygoing companionship. It was almost embarrassing to be truly intimate with your spouse because how could you watch someone floss one minute and the next minute share your deepest passion or tritest of fears? It was almost easier to talk about that sort of thing before you shared a bathroom and a bank account and argued over the packing of the dishwasher.

It's not all bad, this companionable silence, this house-sharing arrangement, this divvying of duties with no major surprises. And after all, there may be children and finances to consider. Maybe we don't feel exhilarated at the thought of seeing our partner tonight and maybe sex has taken a serious back seat to just about everything and anything else, but let's be real.

It's costly to part company, to halve everything you own, to work out who will have the kids for the holidays and pay awkward visits to THFKAH. It's heartbreaking. And didn't we make promises to each other?

Besides, the thought of starting over with someone new is exhausting because, lacking any history together, you'd have to explain the backstory to every remark you make. Do you really want to prepare a new partner for Aunt Ethel, whose funereal pronouncements sound like an artichoke that started to talk? Didn't think so, so let's focus on waking up your current relationship.

A CAMPFIRE

My visual for a fierce conversation is a campfire. Friends and family often gather around the firepit when we're on Orcas Island. Someone says something that is so real we catch our breath. "I've been fantasizing about leaving my job and raising basil instead." Or "Last night I dreamed I was the jockey on the winning horse at the Preakness, but it happened in England and I was only sixteen." Or "Every time I hear that song, it takes me back to the worst moment of my life. It was when . . ."

We are thinking, *Did I hear that right? Did she really say that?* Quickly followed by, *What a privilege it is to be trusted with this disclosure. What might I share that is equally honest?*

We each add a log to the fire and the little campfire becomes a blaze.

Anyone who has ever been camping understands the importance of tending the fire. Don't let it die down, don't let it go out. Add another log.

In *The Other People*, a dark and atmospheric psychological thriller about a missing girl and her father who won't give up hope of finding her, C. J. Tudor describes the central character's failure to realize what a stranger his wife had become:

> It wasn't that they didn't love each other. Once, they had loved each other seriously, relentlessly. But passionate love always dims. It has to. Like anything else, love must evolve. To survive, it needs to smolder, not rage. But you still need to tend it, to keep it throwing out warmth. Be too neglectful, for too long, and the fire goes out completely, leaving you raking through the ashes, searching for that spark you once had.

Connecting at a deep level is about revealing to each other a whole new level of otherness, stripping down to our souls, tending the fire so that it doesn't go out. Think of each conversation as adding a log to your campfire.

Do some of your conversations pour water on the fire? Did the person you married turn off at some point? Did you? Are you living beside each other rather than with each other? Has the fire gone out one missing conversation at a time?

Fierce love requires that we keep the fire going along the way.

When you think of fierce love, think of passion, authenticity, courage, connection. Think relationship at its best. Fierce love is a fast-acting antivenom to the relationship-as-usual mode of high task/low intimacy, hidden agendas, blame, settling for mediocrity, indifference, not really asking, not really listening, passive aggression, and excessive use of avoidance tactics.

> Fierce love is a fast-acting antivenom to the relationship-as-usual mode.

There are additional characteristics of fierce love too. Fierce love . . .

- is rational *and* emotional,
- invites radical transparency,
- lends small gestures great importance,
- is assured and unselfconscious,
- desires and values,
- exists between equal partners,
- is sustainable and subtle,
- is interesting and unadorned,
- often defers,
- evokes home and supports the complexity of relationships,
- values relationship over things,
- doesn't always agree but always understands, and
- overlooks small imperfections.

Speaking of imperfections, *A Man Called Ove* by Fredrik Backman made me laugh and cry and sometimes both at the same time. The book is about an old man and his journey from his simple childhood in Sweden to a struggling life after losing his wife, Sonja, to cancer. Backman wrote:

"Loving someone is like moving into a house," Sonja used to say. "At first you fall in love with all the new things, amazed every morning that all this belongs to you, as if fearing that someone would suddenly come rushing in through the door to explain that a terrible mistake had been made, you weren't actually supposed to live in a wonderful place like this. Then over the years the walls become weathered, the wood splinters here and there, and you start to love that house not so much because of all its perfection, but rather for its imperfections. You get to know all the nooks and crannies. How to avoid getting the key caught in the lock when it's cold outside. Which of the floorboards flex slightly when one steps on them or exactly how to open the wardrobe doors without them creaking. These are the little secrets that make it your home."

So what transformations can you reasonably expect when your conversations are fierce? You can add to the following list, personalize it. For example, would you like to stop feeling lonely in your relationship and instead feel happy in each other's company?

When you consider these transformations and characteristics, what would you like to experience more of? Write down what comes to mind. This is you coming out from behind yourself—with yourself—and making it real.

If you believe that you cannot have the conversations you and your partner have been avoiding unless you are in the presence of a marriage counselor or at a couples' retreat while a third-party peacemaker helps you engage in, manage, cope with, and productively resolve your differences in a safe and respectful environment, I want to change your mind.

This isn't to say that facilitated conversations can't be helpful. They can. But if that's the only setting in which you and your partner can have the conversations you want and need to take place, you're in trouble. Imagine the difference one courageous conversation can make.

You can do this!

FROM X TO Y:
WHAT FIERCE LOVE TRANSFORMS

(X) Before Fierce Love	(Y) Practicing Fierce Love
Doing just enough to maintain the illusion that everything is okay. Focusing on not making things worse rather than improving them. Settling for mediocrity. Learning to limp comfortably.	Consciously nurturing love every day. Keeping it real. Unabashed commitment to creating an exceptional relationship. Deciding to remove the rocks from your shoes.
Hoping and trying to change your partner. Believing that he or she is your problem to solve and that if he/she were different, you'd be happy.	Working on yourself and trusting your partner is able to work on him/herself. Embracing accountability. If it's to be, it's up to me.
A "me versus you" relationship. Game playing, passive aggressive behavior, blaming, manipulation, attempts to get your way. "It's all about me and you need to conform. Your job is to make me happy."	A high level of alignment, collaboration, and partnership within the relationship and the mutual fulfillment that goes with it. "It's about both of us. Neither of us is most important. What can I do to support you?"
Beating around the bush, dancing around the subject, skirting the issues (insert your favorite metaphor here). No one engages. Nothing changes. "What's wrong?" "I don't want to talk about it."	Naming and addressing the issues at the heart of your relationship, truthfully and effectively. Generating impetus for action, for change. "I'm upset about . . . concerned about . . . excited about . . ." "Okay, let's talk."
Blaming. Entrenched victim mode. Abandonment of individual goals. "If you weren't such a jerk . . . You're the reason I'm unhappy, the reason I can't . . ."	Deep-seated accountability. Goals achieved. "I see where I contributed to this problem. Help me think through what I need to do differently."
No shared, compelling vision or values. Competing goals and action plans. Drama, drudgery, struggle, confusion, exhaustion. "I'm tired of beating my head against the wall. Clearly, what's important to me isn't important to you. I give up."	Shared vision and values. Clarity regarding, "Where are we going? Why are we going there? How are we going to get there?" The fog lifts as a result. "Given that one of our goals is ___, what do you see as the next step we need to take?"

A relationship based primarily on paying the bills. High level of dissatisfaction. Difficulty maintaining intimacy. "You wanted a bigger house. I didn't. Now we can't even afford date nights. I hope you're happy."	A relationship that extends beyond financial survival. Both people feel seen and heard. Increased intimacy. "We may not be in our ultimate dream house, but my home is wherever you are. Let's do something fun this weekend."
Stalled personal growth. Individual stagnation. Sleepwalking through the marriage. Business as usual. "I'm bored with my job. I'm bored with you. I'm bored with myself. My life seems to be taking forever."	Shared enthusiasm for personal growth; shared responsibility for achieving a new normal that works for both people. "Congratulations on your promotion! Let's celebrate. By the way, I just signed up for that art class I told you about."
Sex is rare, rote, selfish, faked, nothing new, over quickly. No foreplay, no afterplay, no feeling of intimacy. "I don't like my body. I don't like his/her body. I'm not in the mood. Turn out the light. Get this over with."	Lovemaking is spontaneous, generous, honest, inventive, savored, preceded by touches and glances throughout the day and leaves a feeling of deep connection. "I love us, including our imperfections. I love feeling so close to you."

In part 3 I will walk you through the conversations that will help you and your partner connect at a deep level and enrich your relationship. In the meantime, if you ask yourself what is going to stop you from floating further apart from each other because clearly you are missing an anchor, the answer is a conversation. Certainly more than one, but you have to at least get started.

Now let's define what *isn't* fierce love.

5

What *Isn't* Fierce Love?

The word "divorce" was never spoken. They didn't need to. They were already retreating, ending their marriage stealthily, slipping away from each other so slowly that neither even noticed the other one was disappearing.

—C. J. TUDOR, *THE OTHER PEOPLE*

A dear friend in Australia sent me an email that broke my heart. I had asked her about her relatively new marriage to Dan. Here was her reply:

Ahh, you see sometimes I feel sad. And I feel a great pressure to be perpetually happy (not from you! just in the air) so I avoid contacting you in case I bring you down. This morning I can't hold it in anymore. I find a heaviness deep down in my heart regarding Dan. I expect too much and I'm reminding myself to be grateful for what I have.

I knew what he was like when I married him, but I wrote a romance movie and cast him in an impossible role, so I simply must grow up and face the facts. And that's the present discomfort.

My leading man can be silent and implacable. All those supportive, encouraging things in a conversation or life like a nod or a smile or a "wow" or a "mmm" or a sparkle in the eye are missing. I knew he doesn't smile easily or react. Our kisses are dry little pecks. His face never lights up from inside when he sees me. He forces smiles sometimes just to please me.

Do you think I've married someone who actually doesn't like me? That's how it feels although he says the opposite. I've been trying to kiss him deeply and with emotion but he gets embarrassed and resentful and doesn't like it so I've given up.

He says he shouldn't have to say or do anything to indicate he's heard me or he's interested, but I find it like pouring water into cracked, dry earth. My offerings vanish without a trace. I suspect he would prefer silence. He is very polite and asks polite questions. And if the conversation is the relationship I get lonely. I knew he doesn't like romance, doesn't need affection or intimacy.

I remind myself he's excellent about doing practical things and maybe that's how he expresses his love. He *is* supporting me financially and he'll drive me anywhere. And he gets excited talking about money and his work and that's fun. I just miss feeling loved in the way I understand it. I've never met a man who wants nothing from me. I feel unnecessary.

Countless women can relate to this. And men as well. Why is it that we knew marrying someone was a serious risk, but we did it anyway? I remember asking a friend why she was going to marry someone who seemed like a bad match to me, and she said, "Because he asked me to." As she said that, the look on her face told both of us that she knew this might not be a good idea. She married him. They divorced two years later.

In true-crime shows, at some point the narrator says something like, "Mary didn't want to believe that Mark would do something like that again. She hoped things would calm down and his anger did seem to subside. But there had been signs . . ."

Indeed, there had! There are lessons to be learned wherever we look, which is not to suggest that we learn those lessons. We need to pay attention. There had been signs for my friend. Sadly, she ignored them and is miserable.

I've received guidance from literal signs. Following an argument with my husband, as I was driving, I asked for a message. I looked up and there it was. Yield. I've also received Merge, Stop, and Detour, which were surprisingly useful.

Maya Angelou said, "When someone shows you who they are, believe them the first time." What we do is who we are. When someone says, "That's not me," after doing something or saying something hurtful, they are mistaken. That is them. That is exactly them or at least a part of them, and it may be a part of them that you do not want in your life.

You can't change people. This is why it is so important to do all you can to connect with them at a deep level *before* you marry or start a family. When someone does or says something that doesn't feel right and your instincts tell you something is up, you're right. It is.

SCARLET AND JERRY

On a beautiful October day, Scarlet, one of my most insightful friends, fed her horse and her pygmy pony, then returned to the house. Her husband, Jerry, had left to run errands. For weeks he had been telling her about the women he had befriended at work, the details of their unhappy marriages, a married colleague having an affair with a married man and how he tried to help her. One of the women had even asked Jerry to attend a Yo-Yo Ma concert with her, which seemed odd to Scarlet—odd and inappropriate. Invite a married man out for the evening? Who does that? Also, Jerry had been irritated with Scarlet lately. Nothing she said or did was right. A thought persisted. Things weren't adding up.

Jerry's laptop was on the kitchen table. Scarlet glanced at her husband's emails, open on his laptop, and couldn't resist taking a look. When she sat down and scrolled through his email history, she saw that he had been emailing a coworker with sexually explicit content about past love affairs. Months later, after yet another failed conversation with her husband, Scarlet told me, "I am married to a man I don't really know, and it may be quite some time before I feel like I do know him."

The thing is, she *did* know him. When they were dating, he told her that he enjoyed sleepovers with former lovers from time to time. No sex, just cuddling. *Right!* She said that wouldn't work for her, and she hoped this desire of his would fade away. It didn't and after a year of struggling, they divorced.

THERE WERE SIGNS

Early in another friend's marriage, her husband insisted that he do his own laundry and made it clear that he didn't like to be asked where he was going. Those were flashing neon signs, which she missed completely.

Another friend married a woman who took neediness to a whole new level. When they were dating, he liked the idea of helping her resolve problems in her life. Turned out that *she* was the problem. Her need for high drama led to one catastrophe after another. Eventually he developed compassion fatigue and checked out emotionally, then legally.

Alison Lurie described the flashing red sign of self-absorption in her novel *Foreign Affairs*:

> Perhaps you don't have to interest her, as long as you are sufficiently interested *in* her. . . . On the first date, he talks to impress you. And talks and talks. You learn what he does, major milestones of success, perhaps his history of relationships that ended when he walked away, not her. He doesn't ask about you. You tell yourself that this is typical male posturing and that the second date will be better. And it isn't. Nor is the third. He still seems self-absorbed and not particularly interested in learning about you. But he's attractive and successful and you're three dates into this investment. So you continue.

Self-absorption, possibly narcissistic. Not fun to live with.

The path of our relationships can be littered with warning signs, strung with barbed wire, sign after sign after sign. But we do not want to believe that the relationship we are in is unhealthy, making both of us sicker every day. So we manage not to notice the signs, which is too bad because, as Carl Jung said, "What we do not make conscious emerges later as fate."

What are the signs that a relationship may be headed toward a "suddenly" no one wants?

The Gottman Institute, which employs a research-based approach to relationships, discovered that they could predict whether a couple would divorce with over 90 percent accuracy just by observing them describe their relationship, especially if they disagree with each other about something important. The biggest culprits predicting divorce are criticism, defensiveness, contempt, and stonewalling.

Amen to these! You could also look at the list of characteristics of fierce love in chapter 4 (for example, fierce love overlooks small imperfections) and say that the opposite of those characteristics aren't fierce love and don't bode well for a relationship. But that was *my* list. Yours may be very different.

I am certain of several things, however. If you and your partner aren't being fully truthful with each other, if you withhold what you really think and feel, that most definitely is *not* fierce love. Why is there no connecting? Because we say things we don't mean and mean things we don't say. There remain too many things that you would have liked to say, should have said, have not said, and all those withheld words clutter up your mind.

> Why is there no connecting? Because we say things we don't mean and mean things we don't say.

I sometimes find myself muttering, "Wait! What?" as I listen to yet another person tell me why they didn't say what they wanted to say to their partner. "I wanted to say . . . but it wasn't the right time" or "I hoped that wasn't really how she felt about me" or "I didn't want to ruin the weekend."

What they withheld from their partners, what they wanted to say or ask but didn't, became serious problems. In a new relationship, infatuation doesn't care about obvious signs of trouble, but it should. There is almost always plenty going on right under our noses that we can do something about, only we don't because we literally can't or refuse to see the signs. As Conan O'Brien said, "When all else fails, you always have delusion."

Observing some relationships has been like standing at the low-tide line of a tsunami. *Those two don't like each other.* If a marriage is stagnant, asleep, so are the individuals within it.

> If a marriage is stagnant, asleep, so are the individuals within it.

SPOTTING THE SIGNS

I don't think of myself as unusually gifted in spotting the signs. I think we can all spot them. We just have to stay awake. By that, I don't mean that we are always on the search for a sign that something is wrong in our relationship. It's just that if there is something wrong, we must stop ignoring the signs. We must acknowledge our unease or concern, bring it up to our partner, and ask what's going on.

For me, there's usually a little flicker of nerve endings, a few seconds of silence while I react to what I just heard or saw. I have learned to obey my instinct, to ask questions and be willing to be wrong. Following a recent keynote talk, someone asked me, "What are the signs that you're avoiding a conversation?" My answer: "If you're asking that question, you already know there's a conversation you're avoiding. I suspect there is a flashing neon sign that you've been ignoring. If you're waiting for just the right moment, when you're in the right mood, the sun, moon, and stars are aligned, and the right music is playing in the background, you'll never have it. My counsel to you is have that conversation today."

The following are signs that you may be headed toward an unpleasant "suddenly."

Conflict avoidance

When couples cannot talk about their problems in a healthy way and become entrenched in their opinions, they have the same failed conversations over and over. The relationship becomes emotionally clogged. Friction and frustration grow. Partners feel rejected, like they can't get through to each other. Behaviors associated with conflict avoidance include passive-aggressive actions and withdrawal.

Dishonest conversations

Even the conversations you do have about conflicts aren't honest! This may be the most bizarre, unexpected sign of all. When the conversation that you would rather avoid has actually begun and you're into it, you'd think we would tell it like it is, or at least like we see it. We don't. We downplay the importance and the impact of the issue, pulling back from letting our partner know how upset or concerned we really are.

Triangulating

This is when person A (you) bonds with person B (your best friend) over your frustration with person C (your clueless partner). Rather than talk directly with our partner, we tell a friend, relative, or coworker about the most recent upsetting thing that our partner said or did. There is juice in bringing each other up to date with the latest chapter. "You won't believe what happened last night!" Meanwhile, we look for him/her to screw up again, while person C is oblivious.

Lack of honest feedback

I don't know about you, but I've not yet witnessed a spontaneous recovery from a bad attitude or bad behavior. Without timely, candid feedback, a partner whose behavior or attitude is a problem will continue unchanged. If we withhold our frustration or sadness or anger, the relationship will veer further off course.

Failure to tell our partners how much they are appreciated

It's a huge sign if either of you thinks that a card on your anniversary and a box of chocolates on Valentine's Day is sufficient to convey your love and appreciation. Comments like *Thanks, Okay, Good* don't land. When we have become accustomed to a routine that does not stop now and then to tell our partners specifically what we appreciate about them, no one feels seen, heard, valued. Affairs often begin because someone else is filling that role.

Withholding your frustration

If you haven't told your partner that the relationship is in jeopardy, no fair trying to chuck someone out the door. If you try, your partner—even if aware at some level that things haven't been stellar for quite some time—will likely claim innocence and ignorance. "You told me just last night that you loved me and you thanked me for getting your car fixed, so I thought you were happy." And when we finally reach the end of our rope, we learn that we'll have to have the conversations we've avoided in the past and, to be fair, give our partner another chance.

Allowing the relationship to flatline

The opposite of love isn't hate. It's indifference, lethal neutrality, apathy. You don't care. Instead of energy, there's malaise. Instead of chemistry, there's emptiness. Instead of substance, there's frivolousness. The relationship is all but dead. You and your partner walk around unhappy, unhealthy, on edge, bored, unengaged. Your home is not a happy place. It's just a house.

Prolonged silence

If you remain silent in the presence of hurtful behavior or a lousy attitude, you will become increasingly invisible to yourself and your partner. Yes, you may keep the peace, but with mounting unease you may realize that *you* are what's missing. It is impossible to sustain a happy relationship when you know who you are but regularly default on it. This could look like saying anything from "I love football" when you don't to "I'm perfectly happy staying home to raise the children" when you long to pursue a career that's calling to you, that subject you studied in college.

Living with fear

You sense that your relationship is in jeopardy and immediate action is needed. You could try to take action, but you believe that it would do little good. You feel helpless. You sense that your partner has gone before he or she has gone. You are stressed, afraid.

You and your partner aren't enjoying physical intimacy

Without physical touch, whether having sex or cuddling, we withdraw in other ways. Our lack of intimacy becomes the big thing we don't talk about. It's a tell if, rather than have the conversation, we grow accustomed to the fact that we don't touch. Meanwhile, frustration grows and intimacy exits by the back door and often looks for satisfaction elsewhere.

You and/or your partner are failing to grow personally, failing to adjust or change as needed

It's hard to imagine anyone of substance saying, "I'm so glad I've remained blissfully unaware of how my partner feels about me, enjoyed few insights into my character, and have experienced zero growth as a human being." Those who play it safe, who don't like change, who avoid addressing issues can be found on any street corner. And they are unlikely to be viewed as exemplary partners. Because they aren't.

Allowing your relationship to be at risk

This occurs in part because a relationship professing to value honesty and openness while avoiding tough conversations has no integrity. Relationships in which stated goals and values drive behavior and decisions will weather tough times more successfully than relationships in which behavior is at odds with those goals and values.

To summarize, it's the failed conversations, the missing conversations, the careful conversations that put us on the path to a negative "suddenly." I've endured conversations with people who are so careful they are duller than stumps. There are mud puddles more riveting than the fake smiles on the faces of those whose goal in life is to avoid saying anything controversial.

If we disclosed what we were really thinking and feeling, tears of recognition and amazement might be shed. People would be throwing their arms up in the air, saying, "Yes, yes, yes, that is exactly what I feel too." And it would be the end of loneliness and falsity and the beginning, after all these wasted years, of whatever it is we are supposed to be doing here.

PART 2

The Five Myths
That Mislead
and Derail Us

For every complex human problem, there is a solution that
is neat, simple, and wrong.

—H. L. MENCKEN

Most of us recognize that there are social rules we should
follow. Tip your waiter. Say please and thank you. Don't text while someone
is talking to you. Pick up your dog's poop. I was taught, "If you can't say
anything nice about someone, don't say anything at all." On the other hand,
Alice Roosevelt Longworth famously said, "If you can't say something good
about someone, sit right here by me." You gotta laugh.

In *The Love Song of Miss Queenie Hennessy*, Rachel Joyce wrote, "Perhaps
I took my mother more literally than she intended, but I applied her rules
to my life; after all, we are all searching for them, the rules. We pick them

up from the strangest places, and if they appear once, we can live a whole lifetime by them, regardless of the unhappiness and difficulty they may later bring."

There are times in our lives—at least, I hope there are—when we question the validity of what we've been told rather than adopt others' opinions as our own.

Consider the constellations.

According to Space.com, there are eighty-eight officially recognized constellations in the sky. After the fifteenth century, the southernmost parts of the sky became known and were charted. Furthermore, across the entire sky were large gaps filled chiefly with dim stars. In more recent times people have invented the modern constellations to fill up some of these spaces. We like our dots connected and are happy someone did that for us. A bull? A lion? A scorpion? Looks more like a seahorse to me, but okay, it must be so.

When people agree, often someone smiles and says, "Great minds think alike." Think about this for a minute. If that were true, then nothing new would emerge in this world.

George Bernard Shaw wrote, "The reasonable man adapts himself to the world; the unreasonable one persists in trying to adapt the world to himself. Therefore all progress depends on the unreasonable man." In other words, progress occurs because great minds think differently.

On the topic of love, André Gide wrote,

> I believe that authentic feelings are extremely rare and that the immense majority of human beings are satisfied with conventional sentiments, which they imagine they really experience, but which they adopt without thinking for a minute or questioning their authenticity. People think they are feeling love, desire, disgust, jealousy, and they are living after the fashion of a current model of humanity which is proposed to them from earliest childhood.

There have been some pretty dim stars put forth on the topic of love. We automatically accepted these myths as true because someone we admired told us they were. Trouble is, gradually then suddenly, they led us into a box canyon, so let's consign them to the trash bin.

MYTH 1: You complete me.

MYTH 2: True love is unconditional.

MYTH 3: You must fulfill my list of traits and characteristics.

MYTH 4: If you loved me, you'd know what I want.

MYTH 5: Love is all you need.

So here we go.

6

Myth 1: You Complete Me

You don't need to be in a relationship to be complete.
You're complete because of who you are, not because
of who you're with.
—UNKNOWN

The other day I heard a celebrity who had just gotten
married say that he felt like a jigsaw puzzle whose missing piece had finally
been found. That is an appealing sentiment, yet it can set couples up for
trouble. That missing piece may turn out to be a real piece of work. That
missing piece has a mind of its own. That missing piece may not fit so perfectly over time. That missing piece may mess up your happy life big-time.
And when you look for someone else to complete you, you'll feel empty
when they leave.

This notion of someone completing us is similar to the notion that when
two people marry, they become one. They may become one in the sense of
a spiritual union and they may merge households and incomes, but they
remain distinct individuals. Or should.

BUT THINGS WERE GOING SO WELL . . .

Here's a story that many women, including myself, can relate to:

> There once was a young woman. Let's call her Kate. She has a job as a human resources assistant, a vital position that supports the overall employee experience within her company and documents staff changes, performance reports, and communications.
>
> Kate really likes her job, wants to do well, works hard, and puts in the time necessary to excel. In fact, she arrives at work at 7:30 every morning and often stays a bit late to ensure she's on top of her to-do list. Her boss has noticed her dedication to her career, and she's been put in charge of a culture change initiative. If she does well, she senses she may soon be promoted to human resources specialist. Her self-esteem is healthy.
>
> In addition to her job, she loves her friends. One in particular, Meredith, is her best friend. It's important to both of them to stay in good shape, so on Tuesday and Thursday mornings they meet early before work and go to a yoga class. Once a month Kate meets Meredith and two other friends for dinner. They talk about their lives and encourage one another. Kate knows her friends care about her and value her input. These friendships contribute to her sense of well-being and self-esteem.
>
> Kate also values time alone. One thing she enjoys doing by herself is reading award-winning fiction. She also takes time to be still, to meditate, to get centered. She feels good about the direction her life is taking.
>
> Then she meets *him*. And he lights up her life. He makes her feel brand new. Kate is in love! She wants to be desirable to him and does her best to morph into his ideal mate. For example, even though she doesn't particularly like sports, when he says he wants to spend the weekend watching football, she smiles and says, "I'd love that!"
>
> Kate starts coming to work later, at 9:00 a.m. Her boss asks, "How's that project coming along?" She replies, "It's taking more time than I anticipated." When a colleague asks if Kate can stay late to help out with something, she declines, saying, "I'm meeting my boyfriend."
>
> Meredith calls Monday night and says, "See you in the morning!"

Since being with *him* is her priority, Kate says she can't make it because she's been staying up so late every night that she needs her sleep. The same thing happens on Thursday morning. She doesn't join her friends for their monthly dinner because she has plans with *him*.

There is no more alone time. The culture change initiative is stalled. As Kate realizes she's dropped the ball, she is concerned about what her boss will think. As several months with no yoga pass, Kate starts to notice that she doesn't feel as healthy as usual and her sense of well-being has faded.

When she looks in the mirror, she doesn't love what she sees, doesn't see the Kate that had been so capable, so inspired about her career, so healthy, so close to her friends.

When she turns Meredith down for the fifth time, Meredith says, "I really miss you and I think you're making a mistake, but I won't ask you again." As her friend withdraws, Kate starts to feel the loss, begins to feel isolated. She misses the monthly dinners with her friends. She misses their appreciation of her presence and her input. She misses their conversations, hugs, and laughter. She misses time alone and the feeling of centeredness it had always given her.

Let's summarize:

What's happening with Kate's job and her chances for the promotion? What about her friendship with Meredith? Her other friends? Her physical fitness? Her relationship with herself that has always been enhanced through time alone?

There's a knock on the door. It's *him*. But this time when she opens the door and sees him, instead of "You light up my life," she thinks, "You darken my life!" Instead of "You make me feel brand new," she thinks, "You make me feel used up." What does she do with this relationship? She ends it. "Boy, that was a close call! I almost married that jerk!"

And Kate descends into the pit. Just broke up, job messed up, Meredith not speaking to her, ten pounds overweight. Self-esteem? In the toilet. Now, if she's not careful, what kind of person might be attracted to her while she's in the pit? Another pit person!

Thankfully, Kate refocuses on her work project, calls and apologizes to

Meredith, takes a long walk, hosts the next dinner with friends. Her self-esteem rises, and then one day she meets another *him*. Rinse and repeat.

Why is it that we learn, then forget what we learned and have to learn it all over again? Kate failed to understand something essential. *He* wasn't the problem. He hadn't asked Kate to stop spending time with her friends, stop exercising, stop spending time alone, spend every weekend on the couch watching sports, lose focus on her job. Those things were her call and hers alone.

> Why is it that we learn, then forget what we learned and have to learn it all over again?

Kate's attempts to charm the men in her life required concessions and a certain self-deception. The problem was that Kate made the classic mistake of forsaking herself—her *self*—for another. She set aside the things she loved and the people she cared about in the mistaken belief that if she morphed into her boyfriend's dream girl, life would be sweet. This almost always backfires.

WHAT'S THE MORAL OF THIS STORY?

No one completes us. No one is our missing piece, our other half. We complete ourselves—or fail to. No one else could be successful in that role because each of us is utterly unique. There isn't another you anywhere on this planet. If you somehow feel incomplete, the answers aren't out there somewhere. The answers are in the room. You have them.

You complete me is the myth we must bust to answer the question, *Do I want this relationship?* If you are asking yourself this question, you can't answer it until you can say yes to another question: *Is my life working for me?*

If your life isn't working, you won't be able to tell if he or she is the problem or if you are the problem. Fierce love requires authenticity when what we live is who we really are, when how we spend our days is how we *want* to spend our days. As Annie Dillard wrote, "How we spend our days is how we spend our lives."

We become inauthentic when we trade our real selves for the selves we imagine others desire of us. Attempts to charm others usually require concessions and a certain self-deception. Don't try to charm someone. Focus on being yourself, because there is no other person like you in the world, and eventually the real you will show up. Do you want your partner to be shocked, to feel tricked?

Coming out from behind yourself is part of the search, whether born of panic or courage, for that highly personalized rapture that comes when you feel completely yourself, happy in your own skin. It is a reach for authenticity—a process of individuation—when you cease to compare yourself with others and choose, instead, to live *your* life. It is an opportunity to raise the bar on how you experience your life. It is a deepening of integrity—when who you are and what you live for are brought into alignment. No more tamping down your soul's deepest longings to get approval from others. As André Gide wrote, "It is better to fail at your own life than succeed at someone else's."

Please say the following out loud: *No one and nothing will ever be enough until I am enough.*

To ensure that your life is pleasing to you, or to get it back on track if you've gone off the rails, chapter 11 will provoke the most important conversation you will ever have—a conversation with yourself. Before we go there, let's look at a few more troublesome myths.

7

Myth 2: True Love Is Unconditional

No, I do not want to be loved unconditionally. I want to be shown when I am treating you less than you deserve. I want you to leave if I ever start making you promises I do not see through. Love me for my flaws, yes, but don't you dare ever allow them to hurt you.

—BEAU TAPLIN

Several years ago Lori and Roger joined me for wine and cheese on the deck of my tree house on Orcas Island. The tree house is supported by six Douglas firs, has a ramp that makes it easy to access, and contains all the creature comforts. I am a lucky woman.

I listened as Lori and Roger talked about their young children, their perfect life, but I began to suspect that the most important thing remained to be said. As I refilled their wine glasses, I asked, "So, what aren't you telling me?" There was a long pause and then it came out. A third person had entered their marriage when Roger had an affair. It had been devastating to Lori, and they almost divorced, but they assured me it was over and their marriage was back on track.

After a long pause Lori took Roger's hand, snuggled up to him, looked at me, and said, "We got through it. We can get through anything because we believe in unconditional love." At which point she looked adoringly into Roger's eyes and said, "There is nothing you could ever do that would cause me to leave you."

"Take that back!" I shouted, shocking all three of us. "I suppose you also believe that love conquers all and that love means never having to say you're sorry, which is a total load of crap!" I looked at their startled faces, took a deep breath, and explained.

"Those who say that the greatest gift we can give another is unconditional love haven't thought this through. Love can be crazy, broken, divine, stumbling, sweaty, flawed, beautiful, but unconditional? Stop telling that story. If you two want to stay together, here on this planet, in this lifetime, up close and personal, there should be conditions."

I turned to Lori. "We all make mistakes. We need to forgive and be forgiven, but you just told Roger that there will be no consequences if he cheats again. If he did cheat again, would you happily stay in the marriage? And Roger, would you respect Lori if she stayed with you no matter how badly you behaved? And there's something else I want you to think about, Lori. Have you read *The Giving Tree* by Shel Silverstein to your children?" She nodded.

"Well, according to Wikipedia this book has been described as 'one of the most divisive books in children's literature.' Is the relationship between the boy and the tree positive because 'the tree gives the boy selfless love' or is it negative? Do the boy and the tree have an abusive relationship?"

Again, wide eyes from Lori and Roger.

"I remember reading it to my daughters and wanting to yell at the tree. 'Stop it! Don't give one more branch to that ungrateful brat!'"

Lori looked stunned. Roger looked embarrassed. I continued. "There are two things I want you both to consider. First, we teach others how to treat us. Second, we get what we tolerate.

"If either of you tolerates bad behavior, at some point you deserve what you get. In saying what you just said, Lori, you signaled that, although it would be painful, you wouldn't leave the marriage no matter what Roger did. A relationship without conditions invites martyrdom, yet instead of the gratitude you might think you're owed, you may find yourself alone and confused, because martyrs are no fun to be around.

"Roger shouldn't want that for you. You shouldn't want that for yourself. But if there are no conditions under which you would leave the marriage, then what's to stop Roger from having another affair or from doing other things that would be painful for you?"

> We teach others how to treat us. . . . We get what we tolerate.

Some silences are very loud. I continued.

"I want you to give each other heaping handfuls of love with the caveat that it is conditional, and so I recommend that you both clarify the conditions under which you would no longer want this marriage. Talk about them. Don't list things because you've been told that they should be important to you. This has to be real for you, unique to you. This may sound harsh, but if you want to experience unconditional love, get a dog. They're the best."

I wish I could have listened in on Lori and Roger's ferry ride home.

STOP IT!

Have you ever known someone who was a "giving tree," inexhaustibly obliging? Perhaps you took advantage of that and increased your demands, or perhaps you wanted to get away from them, even judging them to be somewhat pathetic because they either had no goals of their own or made others' goals more important. That person is not a complete person. Not whole. Not strong enough to claim the life he or she wants. And that leaves that person vulnerable to influence from others.

What if you recognize that *you* are a giving tree, that you have essentially martyred yourself to this idea of unconditional love? While it's easy to understand that we get what we tolerate, the challenge comes in figuring out the best way to bring something hurtful to our partner's attention. Most of us make it too complicated.

When we don't like what we are getting, we simply need to say, "Stop it!" In fact, when I am asked about my approach to coaching, I recommend potential clients watch a video on YouTube called "Bob Newhart—Stop It."

(Look it up for fun.) This pretty much sums up my approach. And I hope it made you laugh.

When you tell someone to stop doing or saying hurtful things, they may give you their reasons for their bad behavior. "I yelled at you because I'm under a lot of stress at work." "I'm sorry I said you were stupid. I'm just tired of explaining . . ." Don't be too quick to forgive them. We all have plenty of reasons for behaving badly, but we can either have what we say we want, or we can have all our reasons why we don't have what we want. For example, we say we want a loving relationship and yet we say hurtful things, which we justify with our reasons. It doesn't work like that. Reasons or results. We can't have both. We have to choose, and conditions need to be clarified.

In chapter 17 I'll give you guidelines for having this conversation. In part 3 you and your partner will have a conversation about conditions, but take a few minutes now to begin the list of what is essential for your continued happiness and commitment in a relationship.

8

Myth 3: You Must Fulfill My List

My ideal mate . . . will speak French, raise horses, solve
mathematical paradoxes in his spare time, and write poems,
paying strict attention to meter.
—EDITH PEARLMAN, *HONEYDEW*

A friend showed me a dating spreadsheet she created.
Down the left side was a column of traits. Across the top were the names of
the men she was dating, each in a different color with ticks in boxes down
the column. Here are the traits, just as she wrote them, with my initial
reaction to some of them in italics:

Must be six feet two inches tall. *(Would you say no to five feet ten or six
feet one?)*
Great family relations with ex, kids, immediate family.
Adores me. *(Yuck, not a fan of the word.)*
Believe and achieve abundance. *(Are we talking money here?)*
Driven.
Spiritual. *(Up for interpretation.)*

Balanced. *(Ditto.)*

Open to new ideas.

Curious and loves to learn.

Loves to travel.

Supportive of me, my work, my ideas.

Loves animals.

Positive.

Generous—with his love, time, stuff.

Been in therapy successfully. *(If he's all these other things, would he have required therapy?)*

Gets body/health issues: ex-professional athlete. *(Oh, come on! How about just healthy and fit?)*

Creative.

Loyal.

Trustworthy.

Self-confident.

Understanding. *(What must he understand?)*

Passionate.

Emotionally available.

Charming.

Attractive heart, mind, physical.

Optimistic, not a "worry personality."

Comfortable in various environments/people.

Authentic self.

Great smile, good teeth.

Single and available for relationship. *(Well, duh!)*

"Man dominant" instead of boy. *(What the heck does this mean?)*

Nurturing.

Thoughtful, considerate.

Sensitive.

Knows "I am the one." *(A little self-absorbed maybe?)*

Physically compatible.

Laughs with me, makes me laugh.

Open-minded.

Charitable.

Secure.

Shares interest in taste and architecture and design.

Knows where true strength and power lie and lives. *(I'll bite. Where do they live?)*

Humble/humility. *(Unlike you?)*

Trusts himself.

Responsible.

Giver/likes to give gifts.

Innate ability for heart-to-heart communication.

Ready and available to have deeply intimate relationship.

Energy/soul connection.

Interdependent.

Able to learn relationship lessons with me.

Inspires me to be a better person.

My jaw dropped to the floor about halfway through the list. First, this is a painfully long list. Second, some of these items are disturbing. Some are mysterious. Most are up for interpretation. If I dated someone and saw they had a list like this, I'd run for the hills.

We each have a list of traits and shared interests that are important, and when we recognize that the drift is big with a particular person, we need to turn them loose. For example, if a man I was considering dating dismissed a concern I had about my dog's health or well-being by saying "It's just a dog," I'd be gone.

The point is that no one could be all the things on my friend's list. Nobody would *want* to be all those things. You'd have to be a saint, which in my view would be something of a bore.

I laughed when a friend, whose Southern upbringing resulted in strong opinions about proper behavior, showed me the much shorter list she had given the man she was dating:

• Do not spit in front of me or in public. Ever.
• Do not fart in my presence.
• Do not use a toothpick in public.
• Don't chew with your mouth open.

61

- Do not pare your fingernails in public.
- Do not tell me how hot another woman is.
- Your Star Wars Battle of the Death Star floor lamp is not allowed in my house.

I'm not making this up.

UNREALISTIC EXPECTATIONS

You could spend a lifetime running from one relationship to another, looking for someone who fulfills your list. Like a carton of milk, when the person you're dating goes sour, you throw them out and get a fresh one. Even if you try something a bit different, like oat milk or almond milk, it sours like the one before. Another ending, a divorce, an "It's not you, it's me." Or "It's not me, it's you." Whatever. It ages you. These failures, these dreams, become nightmares. And yet you continue. Chasing your fantasy. Hoping your fatigue doesn't show, dodging questions about why your relationship failed, why your marriage ended. Because you realize you have told that story more than once.

Still we persist. Everything will be perfect with the right man or woman, except you keep discovering that the grass that looks so green on the other side of the fence is Astroturf.

No relationship is perfect. When you commit to someone, you commit to an imperfect person with a list of issues you'll be grappling with for a long time. Some are problems you can live with. On the other hand, if you have a low threshold of annoyance, what behaviors in a partner would make the relationship intolerable?

In addition to expecting someone to fulfill your unrealistic expectations, there's another problem with lists. Making a list and sticking to it can cause you to miss out on some wonderful possibilities. Expectations can fall away when we are surprised by an unlikely attraction. Love is not susceptible to logic.

In *The Nix*, Nathan Hill wrote: "People love each other for many reasons, not all of them good. They love each other because it's easy. Or because they're used to it. Or because they've given up. Or because they're scared." It's impossible to explain romantic attachment.

Make a list of the traits and characteristics you desire in a partner, then *be* your list.

There are also cultural differences between partners. Some countries have different standards on acceptable behavior. For example, affairs are often accepted in France—no big deal. Some set the bar too high. In *The Razor's Edge*, W. Somerset Maugham wrote this wonderful line: "American women expect to find in their husbands a perfection that English women only hope to find in their butlers."

Go ahead and make a list of the traits and characteristics you desire in a partner, then *be* your list. For example, I used to view "Summons" by Robert Francis as my list.

> Keep me from going to sleep too soon
> Or if I go to sleep too soon
> Come wake me up. Come any hour
> Of night. Come whistling up the road.
> Stomp on the porch. Bang on the door.
> Make me get out of bed and come
> And let you in and light a light.
> Tell me the northern lights are on
> And make me look. Or tell me clouds
> Are doing something to the moon
> They never did before, and show me.
> See that I see. Talk to me till
> I'm half as wide awake as you
> And start to dress wondering why
> I ever went to bed at all.
> Tell me the walking is superb.
> Not only tell me but persuade me.
> You know I'm not too hard persuaded.

I would love this in a companion, and it would be a bonus if he were a falconer, a park ranger, a wildlife photographer, or Sting, but I can't put any of this on someone else. I must keep myself from going to sleep too soon. I must get myself out of bed and go outside and light a light. And when I do these things, like the Scarecrow and the Tin Man, I find that I already had the thing I sought all along. If I am waiting and hoping for someone else to wake me, I could end up sleeping the years away.

9

Myth 4: If You Loved Me, You'd Know

Tell me why. Tell me how. Tell me what I don't know. Tell me something, tell me anything, but please tell me what it is you're keeping from me.

—BELLA POLLEN, *THE SUMMER OF THE BEAR*

If you loved me, you'd know I need a hug. You'd know my feelings are hurt. You'd know I'm exhausted and need help. You'd know you should have asked me before you volunteered to host Thanksgiving at our house. If you loved me, you'd know I need you to put your arms around me and tell me you love me.

But we don't know. As Miles Davis said, "If you understood everything I said, you'd be me."

I've admitted to friends and family that sometimes you have to hit me over the head with a two-by-four for me to get a message, because I truly do not know what you are saying, what you mean, what you want. Perhaps I am dense. Several years ago I confessed this to Ed, whom I've known since high school. We were driving back to my house after a sumptuous breakfast at Salish Lodge, overlooking Snoqualmie Falls, about a thirty-minute drive from Seattle. Ed said, "I don't understand why you didn't remarry after your divorce. There must be plenty of guys who would be interested."

"Thanks for the compliment," I said. "Maybe there are, but I don't usually notice if someone is attracted to me in that way. A man would practically have to throw himself across my windshield for me to get the message."

After another mile or so, Ed said, "Pull over, please."

I looked at him, questioning. "You okay?"

"I'm fine," he said. I pulled over.

He got out, went around to my side of the car and draped his six-foot-three-inch body across the windshield, smiling broadly.

That was one of the most wonderful, memorable things a man has ever done for me. So funny, so clear. And if he hadn't done it, I would not have guessed his feelings, not even close.

The point is, when two people are not speaking clearly or not speaking at all, one could ask the other, "Are you hoping to transmit your thoughts to me telepathically?" Expecting someone to know what we want and need is pretty silly, given that *you* don't even know what you want half the time. Might it be easier to simply ask?

Do you want to go to a movie? Okay, then. Say so. And when asked what movie you want to see, name it. Don't say, "I don't know, what do you want to see?" Say, "I'd like to go see *Parasite* or *Nomadland* or *Marriage Story* or *Once Upon a Time in Hollywood* or . . .")

Parade's End is a novel set against the backdrop of World War I. It looks at Christopher Tietjens and his marriage, which struggles from the start. The author, Ford Madox Ford, captured what Ms. Wannop and Christopher Tietjens are thinking but not saying.

> She wanted to say: "I am falling at your feet. My arms are embracing your knees!"
>
> Actually she said: "I suppose it is proper to celebrate together today!" . . .
>
> She knew that he desired to say, "I hold you in my arms. My lips are on your forehead. Your breasts are being hurt by my chest!" [Modern translation: he wanted to say that he was crushin' on her; he was hot for her.]
>
> He said: "Who have you got in the dining-room?"

We are so used to not saying what we are really thinking that we don't even catch ourselves in the act. I'd like us to wake up and notice how often we withhold what we're thinking and feeling and how this affects our relationships.

Dr. Gary Chapman, author of *The 5 Love Languages*, says the key to a lasting relationship is learning our partner's love language. I found this book truly useful, though I have a few questions. One of the love languages is giving gifts. In other words, I feel loved when you give me gifts. Or you feel loved when I give you gifts.

I have seen this arrangement crash and burn. Especially if the way we patch up a fight is to give a gift. I agree with Hafiz, a Persian poet who celebrated love, wine, and nature. He wrote, "The idiot's warehouse / Is always full." Gifts are lovely, but if we don't have the conversation about the fight we just had, we will likely have it again. And our gift-giving may end up breaking the bank.

> We are so used to not saying what we are really thinking that we don't even catch ourselves in the act.

Although all five love languages—physical touch, quality time, words of affirmation, acts of service, gifts—can help us feel loved, if there is a persistent silence consisting of all the things we can't talk about, that feeling will be temporary.

The mistake we make is hanging out in hope that our partner will intuit what we want and need at any given time. Don't bet on that. We must tell them.

HOW TO BE WITH ME

We begin to teach people what matters to us, what we require from the moment we meet them. I'm not suggesting we teach people how to *be*. That would be about control and manipulation. This is about teaching people, especially our partners, how to be with *me*.

The point is—if you want something from me, *tell me*! If you're upset with me, *tell me*! If there's something you want me to do or stop doing, *tell me*! If I said something that didn't go down well with you, stop the conversation right then and there and *tell me*! And if you're happy with me, *tell me*!

The problem when we wait until later in the relationship to have these conversations is that we have to deal with all the buildup of resentment and anger inside and the massive amount of retraining that needs to take place. The sooner we take a stand the easier it will be—and the kinder we will be when we deliver the message.

10

Myth 5: Love Is All You Need

[Regarding marriage,] both people need to care deeply about the other person, to put the other's needs before their own, and to make a daily commitment to that person to stick it out.
—ALESSANDRA TORRE, *BLINDFOLDED INNOCENCE*

I'm a Beatles fan from way back and love the song "All You Need Is Love." Without love, whatever else we have will fail to fulfill us because our typical notions of success won't give us joy, won't lead to a meaningful life. But we need more than love, more than a notion, an ideal, a song. We need clarity about the kind of love we want to experience; clarity about the kind of person with whom we could fall in love. If I were looking for a partner, I'd be looking for a fairly evolved product.

Sometimes what we need is elusive. We are changeable and inscrutable, even to ourselves. We go wrong when we think that love has limitless power, that it will provide what we don't even know we want. We believe that it can save us and that we can save a partner, that we can love them through whatever character flaws they are displaying so that

Even though loving someone won't necessarily change that person, our soul doesn't know this and persists in an impossible endeavor.

they become a far better person, which of course is *our* ideal person, not necessarily a shared goal.

If I were a gambler this is not an outcome I would put money on. Even though loving someone won't necessarily change that person, our soul doesn't know this and persists in an impossible endeavor, even when we suffer and when we pay a price for our failure, which is, of course, not entirely our failure but the other person's.

PEOPLE CHANGE

In Italy, a life prison sentence means lifelong—no chance of parole. Many feel that marriage is a life sentence, that we must pledge to be together till death do us part, promising to love every person our partner is and will become no matter what. This is a beautiful notion, and I am all for doing everything humanly possible to save a struggling marriage. It's just that forever is a long time. What about till cheating doth us part? Or abuse of any kind? What if your spouse becomes a meth addict or an alcoholic and no amount of treatment helps?

What if your roads significantly diverge? *Significantly.* People do change, want different things. That's natural, to be expected. No doubt you will do your best to honor and accommodate conflicting goals, at least that's what I hope you'd do. But what if your roads have diverged to the point where what you and your partner want is truly incompatible?

I am not suggesting a marriage of convenience. Far from it. I *am* suggesting that the notion "All you need is love" is a myth because you can love someone—really, really love them—and not make a go of the relationship because you discover that your partner holds values in direct opposition to yours or behaves in ways that hurt you and others.

Perhaps you are philanthropic and want to give back to your community, while your spouse takes unfair and illegal advantage of your community and expects you to look the other way. Perhaps you married and planned to take turns supporting each other to get the degrees or skills needed for your desired professions. But you supported your spouse for ten years, your turn hasn't come, and your spouse refuses to honor his or her end of the bargain. You dreamed of becoming a biologist, a lawyer, a horticulturist, a nurse, but that's no longer in the cards. Your dream isn't deferred. It's denied. You played your part for all these years, but the agreement was unilaterally revoked. What you need is unavailable, out of reach. Is that okay?

There is, of course, a difference between *want* and *need*. I want plenty of things I don't need. You probably do too. What you *need*, that craving that won't go away, whether it's an experience or an accomplishment, should not be dismissed as unimportant or selfish. What you need matters because, to the degree that it is missing, you are going hungry.

Of course, what we need will be different for each of us. I don't have a wildly long list. In addition to love, one of my nonnegotiables is good grammar. For me, bad grammar is a serious turnoff. To you that may seem ridiculous or snobby, but the truth is, as soon as I hear someone say, "Me and her . . ." I back away. I am both solitary and social, so in addition to love, I need heaping handfuls of solitude, meaningful work, my dogs (we balance out our character defects), a few close friends, time with family, art supplies, a vegetable garden, great music that drops me into a place where I write my best stuff, good red wine, chocolate, and a valid passport. I also need to give back, to help, to make a difference. Doing so gives me joy.

My partner must hold similar values to mine, must be mentally and physically active and happy to explore the world with me, must behave in ways that make me proud of him, and must allow me the solitude I require for writing and thinking. (And, of course, he must love dogs. You knew that.)

What comes up for you? Would you be happy with a person of limited palette, someone whose lifestyle could be described as early ransack, someone who is committed to living life on the couch in front of the TV? Or do you have something else in mind?

Take a few minutes to think about what you need in addition to love and write those things down.

Remember, if you are missing things you hunger for, part of you is starving, so think about how you can get at least a bit of them into your life as soon as possible. For example, if you crave time alone, plan a retreat for yourself. The first time I did this, I assured my husband that I would return to him refreshed and grounded, and I did. If you have always wanted to paint, sing, or bird-watch, sign up for lessons or join a group. If you have always wanted to give back to the community, look for places that could use your help.

PART 3

The Eight Conversations of Fierce Love

If you can abandon your principles for convenience, or social acceptability, then they are not your principles. They are your costume.

—NITYA PRAKASH

Before diving into the conversations I'm encouraging you to have with your partner, I offer an African greeting and a brief primer on the principles of fierce conversations.

In the Maasai Mara, which to me is one of the most beautiful places on this earth, when two people greet each other, one says *Sawubona*, which means "I see you." The response is *Ngikhona*, which means "I am here." The order is important. It's as if until you see me, I don't exist.

Sawubona. (I see you.)
Ngikhona. (I am here.)

During conversations with a partner, raking our eyes quickly over someone's face is not seeing him or her. Each of the conversations that follow requires that you be fully present, look into your partner's eyes, and slow the conversation down so it can find out what it wants and needs to be about.

Your undivided attention is important because where a conversation begins may not be where it goes, may not be where it ends. If you're not paying attention, you may miss the detour into important territory.

SEVEN PRINCIPLES OF FIERCE CONVERSATIONS

Recall the premise that while no single conversation is guaranteed to change the trajectory of a relationship, any single conversation can. There are principles that can help. I wrote a book with a chapter on each of these principles—*Fierce Conversations*—so if you want a deep dive, that's where you'll find it. But here is a short summary.

Principle 1: Master the courage to interrogate reality.

No plan survives its collision with reality, which has an irritating habit of shifting things at work and at home—with no advance notice. The world changes. Markets and economies change. People change and forget to tell one another. We are all changing all the time. Not only do we neglect to tell others, we are skilled at masking change to ourselves. No wonder relationships disintegrate. Perhaps what we thought was the truth is no longer the truth today.

Principle 2: Come out from behind yourself into the conversation and make it real.

Trust requires persistent identity. You will be trusted when you always come into your conversations as yourself, not to say what you think others want to hear. We are attracted to what is real, to authenticity. Our radar detects its absence. Something within us responds deeply to those who level with us, who don't suggest our compromises for us. When the conversation is real, change often occurs before the conversation has ended.

Principle 3: Be here, prepared to be nowhere else.

One of the greatest gifts we can give another person is the purity of our attention, yet many of us suffer from chronic preoccupation. We have one foot in the work world, one foot in the world of personal growth, and two or three feet in other areas. We may hear every word someone says yet miss the message altogether. Put down your phone, that kind of social shield you pull out and fiddle with when you feel awkward. Close your laptop. Set everything else aside. It will wait for you. Sometimes it's helpful to confess, "I'm sorry. I drifted. I'm back now."

Principle 4: Tackle your toughest challenge today.

Burnout occurs not because we're trying to solve problems but because we've been trying to solve the same problem over and over. If you know something must change, then know that it is you who must change it, and it is going to require a conversation—probably more than one. Identify the problem and focus on solving it. Look for the deepest issue that engages or troubles you. Name it. Come straight to the issue. Get right to the point. *Today.*

Principle 5: Obey your instincts.

Don't just trust your instincts. Obey them. There are things our gut knows long before our intellect catches on. Your radar works perfectly. It's the operator who is in question. An intelligence agent is sending you messages every day, all day. If you ignore those messages, eventually you'll stop getting them. Pay attention.

Principle 6: Take responsibility for your emotional wake.

In your relationship with your partner, there is no trivial comment. Something you don't even remember saying may have left a wound that is still painful. Or perhaps he or she is still grateful to you for something you don't remember saying. Emotional wake is what you remember, what you feel when your partner is gone. The aftermath, aftertaste, or afterglow. An offhand comment can be a powerful diminishment, or it can express appreciation, unfiltered, unqualified. Once we've said it, it's out there. It's not coming back.

Principle 7: Let silence do the heavy lifting.

Native Americans pose the question: "Where in your life did you become uncomfortable with the sweet territory of silence?" Talking does not a conversation make. When there is a whole lot of talking going on, conversations skim the surface. No one engages. Nothing changes. There are insights and emotions that can find you only through and within silence. The more emotionally loaded the subject, the more silence is required.

It would be unreasonable to expect yourself to practice all seven principles on day one, and this brief primer only gives you a taste, not the entire meal. Still, I encourage you to choose the principle you want to focus on for the next thirty days. (I go into a more in-depth plan for this in *Fierce Love: A Journal for Couples*.)

Listen to yourself as you've never listened before. What thoughts, questions, or disappointments in yourself or in your partner are you ignoring? Pay close attention. See if you can overhear yourself

- avoiding the topic,
- changing the subject,
- holding back,
- telling little lies (and big ones),
- being imprecise in your language, or
- being uninteresting, even to yourself.

And at least once today, when something inside you says, "This is an opportunity to be fierce," stop for a moment, take a deep breath, and come out from behind yourself into the conversation and make it real.

Say something that is true for you.

You can't control what happens; it could go well or it could get a little bumpy, but you will have been real. And that's saying something! You will have said at least one real thing today, one thing that was real for you.

We sometimes mourn the wasted words that passed for conversations with important people from our past. If we had been real, if we had asked one another what we were thinking and feeling, a new trajectory would have been revealed and we would have grown. That's what I want for you. That would be a *great* beginning.

Now, let's explore the conversations that will help you create love—one conversation at a time. Each chapter ends with words you could say. Just absorb them and use your own words. You be *you*.

11

Conversation 1: Do I Want This Relationship?

The indispensable first step to getting the things you want out of life is this: Decide what you want.
—BEN STEIN

Today, as you look at the person you are with, even if you're committed to staying in your relationship no matter what, you may quietly be asking yourself, *Is this the person I want to go through challenging times with for the rest of my life?* Because one thing's for sure. You'll go through challenging times.

While this is an important question, the moment of truth is when you ask a different question, which I suggested in an earlier chapter. Am I the person I was meant to be? Is my life an expression of my values, my priorities?

If you recall the idea that all conversations are with yourself and sometimes they involve other people, well, this conversation is most definitely with yourself. You will eventually engage your partner in this and all of the following conversations, but first the great, all-powerful Oz is going to come out from behind the curtain and chat with you honestly and boldly.

Remember Kate and *him* and the guy after him and possibly the one

Am I the person I was meant to be?

after that? Kate's view of him changed from *You light up my life* to *You darken my life* because before him, she had been happy with her life. During the relationship she gave up the activities that had been important to her, and eventually she felt the loss. When the relationship ended, she got her life back and then met another *him*, starting the doomed cycle all over again.

Someday I can imagine Kate saying, "I married the wrong guy three times." But in all likelihood, who she became during her relationships was the problem, not the men in her life. When we don't feel good about ourselves, we cast that shadow over those nearby, which clouds our judgment about the relationship.

A word about compromise. Some is necessary. But if you realize that your life is an endless, ongoing compromise and is no longer (or never was) the life you had in mind, you've gone too far.

I'm not suggesting that a new person can't point us toward wonderful things. A friend of mine met a man who meditates. Wanting to impress him, she told a Tai Chi instructor she wanted a crash course. He refused. "Crash and Tai Chi don't work." She laughed and signed up. Today she teaches Tai Chi herself and her relationship with the man who prompted her to take it up is thriving.

What I want you to understand is that the most important relationship in your life, the one you'll have, like it or not, until the day you die, is with yourself. I want you to like it.

This begins with a reality check. I admit to fantasizing from time to time about how my life would be different if I lived somewhere else. A ranch in Montana, a beach house in Maui. I imagine that if I moved to a thatched cottage in an English village to be near dear friends, I'd live a different life. Long walks with my dogs, thinking deep thoughts as I gaze out over the English countryside. Or reading beside the fire, a hearty soup simmering on the AGA. Or that if I moved to a condo in Pike Place Market in the heart of Seattle, I'd get out more, go to the Seattle Art Museum, socialize. Or that if . . . You get the drift.

In fact, I did move from a wonderful home in the suburbs to a Pike Place Market condo in downtown Seattle. I lasted three years, then hightailed it back to the burbs where my dogs have a yard and I have the privacy, solitude, and quietude that suits me. I'm a country mouse, not a city mouse.

We take ourselves with us wherever we are, love what we love, who we love, how we love. A new place doesn't change who we are at our core.

As I said earlier, no one and no thing will ever be enough until *you* are enough, and you will never be enough until you are happy and successful in your own life. By *success* I don't mean stomping the competition and ending up all alone on top of some mythical heap. That's just a booby prize we go after because nobody ever told us what success really is. We will be successful when there is complete alignment between who we are or wish to become and what we live. This is more important than most of us realize.

I learned something years ago that surprised me: the study of psycho-neuroimmunology has found that although our immune systems are affected by lifestyle (smoking, drinking to excess, no exercise, etc.), the most important indicator of our health is the amount of integrity with which we live our lives. For example, if I say that family matters most to me and yet I'm not spending quality time with my family, I am out of integrity. Depending on how large the gap is between what I say I believe and how I actually behave, my immune system weakens. If I recognize this and change my behavior, my immune system strengthens. *Immediately.*

> We will be successful when there is complete alignment between who we are or wish to become and what we live.

I think most of us sense that this is true. It's certainly true for me. For example, I believe and tell others that it's important for me to spend time in nature, to walk, to hike. I also know that when I'm doing the couch potato routine, I don't feel good about myself and probably don't feel good physically. I catch a cold, notice stiffness in my joints. I'm out of integrity. My immune system is weakening.

So the question "Am I the person I was meant to be?" is a big deal. Are the things I say I value and what I am actually doing in alignment? If not, what do I need to do to correct this?

Our lives can be deadly boring or a profound experience of humanity, intimacy, and connection. The best lives apply head, heart, and hands to living an attentive, balanced, joyful life. And this requires a unique perspective. *Yours.* No one else can or should design your life for you. We will find it nearly impossible to connect with the one we love or hope to love until we have connected with ourselves, our real selves. We can't let others into our real life if there isn't one. We are not authentic if we are faking what we think others expect of us and it isn't what we desire. I've often wondered why humans are the only animals who often refuse to be themselves.

HAVE YOU SETTLED ON YOUR SIGNATURE?

Do you remember junior high school when you experimented with your signature? For me, it was dotting the *i*'s with *o*'s, lots of loops and curves. This was an important phase of playing with possible identities, literally creating a signature that matched your picture of yourself and how you wanted others to view you. (Note: I won a prize in first grade for the best handwriting. The prize was two chickens and a rooster. I'm not making this up. They did things like that in Tennessee when I was a little girl. My handwriting has gone seriously downhill since then. No more chickens for me.)

Now your signature is automatic and requires no thought or effort, like driving a familiar route. You end up somewhere with little memory of how you got there. We're great drivers, often zooming along on automatic pilot, not enjoying the journey all that much. It is unsettling when we begin to wonder if the road we're on will take us where we want to go.

Even more disturbing, many people are not only asleep at the wheel but have no compelling destination in mind. Their lives have no signature.

I often ride the ferry to Orcas Island, and upon arrival there is an announcement. "We have reached our destination. All passengers must disembark." I always have the same thought: *Ain't that the truth. When I reach the end of my journey, no matter how much I love my life and this earth, I'll have to disembark.* This prompts a check-in with myself.

The process of clarifying you to yourself may seem daunting, but you can start almost anywhere. The facets of your life are like pieces of a kaleidoscope—all different, all connected, all influencing the others. When a single piece shifts, the entire picture changes dramatically. In clarifying one thing that our lives require and in taking the first step needed to make it happen, things are set in motion.

Do you experience more happy than sad, more peace than war, more freedom than containment? Have you had a good laugh lately? Does "real" win out, triumph over illusion, affectation, pretense? What is the highest-priority item missing from your life? Perhaps you're a Renaissance person who isn't happy unless you have two or three irons in the fire. That's fine. Choose those irons and thrust them into the coals. The goal is to increase your joy, for you to feel more yourself, not so you will be attractive to others but so you will be attractive to yourself.

To get started on a check-in with yourself, as you read the questions below, write down the first things that come to mind.

- Are my interests and priorities shifting? If yes, how?
- What facets of myself have lain dormant or have never seen the light of day?
- Is there an area I care about that is conspicuously absent? If so, what is it?
- To what degree am I realizing my full potential?
- To what degree is there value and meaning in my life?
- What am I called to do?
- What activities have heart for me?
- What's the most fun thing I'm going to do today?
- If I am stressed, is this stress really worth it?
- What can I do to get more of what I want and need in my life?

To help you think even deeper and further, I recommend writing your stump speech, a term used today to describe a candidate's standard speech delivered day after day during a typical political campaign. But in the nineteenth century, the phrase held a much more colorful meaning. Stump speeches got their name for a good reason: they would often be delivered by candidates who literally stood atop a tree stump. Your stump speech becomes the clear message that you will share repeatedly with yourself, your partner, family, friends, with anyone who wants to know you well.

I offer my stump speech as an example later in this chapter, but don't copy mine. What's important is that you concern yourself with *you*, yourself, not the relationship between you and X. You'll answer four questions:

1. Where am I going?
2. Why am I going there?
3. Who is going with me?
4. How will I get there?

Notice that "Who is going with me?" is the third question, not the first. It's important not to get these out of order. *What* you do with your life must be number one, not *who* you do it with.

I remember a woman telling me the story of her life before Jack, during Jack, and after Jack. If we are ever to have tranquility and peace of mind, our lives must revolve around a center. Jack was the center of her life. That's not to say that the ones we love aren't at the center of our lives. It's just that they aren't *the* center.

Each of us is on our own path, but it's important that we stop from time to time and ask where our path is taking us, is that really where we want to go, and is it supporting us to be the person we want to be.

So before you write your stump speech, ask yourself, *What labels do I want others to attach to me?* Elizabeth Cady Stanton, the American feminist and women's rights pioneer, said, "I would have girls regard themselves not as adjectives, but as nouns." If you are beautiful, that was the luck of the gene pool, so you don't get credit for it. Wife, mother? Yes, perhaps, but what else? What nouns would you hope might follow your name in conversations about you? If you keep coming up with words like *sweet, kind, generous, strong, sassy,* or *confident,* those are all good, but they are adjectives.

Reach deeper. How about trailblazer, teacher, adventuress, philanthropist, artist, lighthouse? If you could have any labels attached to you, what would they be? A neighbor who makes tinctures and salves from nettles, old-man's beard, and other plants found in the Pacific Northwest describes herself as an alchemist. Love that! And it doesn't hurt that she steeps plants in vodka for a month or two.

Your stump speech may change over time because life is an improvisational life-form, inviting us to redefine and reinvent ourselves for the time and place in which we find ourselves. You can't always foresee the interesting side trips you may take, but where are you headed? How big do you want your life to be? A trajectory and destination are essential for clarity, even though you will make course corrections as wisdom and maturity broaden your perspective and scrub that last shred of inauthenticity off you. So what do you want? What matters to you?

Pull back from your life and look at it as if you're the screenwriter, director, producer, and star. What's the plot? What's the story? What do you want more than anything? What's the conflict? What's the ideal ending? When you get to the end of your life and look back, what would you regret not having done or at least attempted?

Another benefit of clarifying where you are going with your life, the contribution you wish to make, and your ideal future is that it will help you decide what to say yes to and what to say no to. Saying no is important. If you say yes to all invitations and temptations, you won't have room for the big yes that may be around the corner, so if something doesn't fit with the overall direction and purpose of your life, if it will be a distraction, say no.

This exercise requires and deserves time. Ideally, a personal retreat. At a minimum, several hours. Your living room will work just fine—though, if possible, I suggest that you get out of your everyday environment. A change in your literal horizon will boost your ability to see new horizons for your life and career.

Why is it so important to spend time conversing with ourselves? Because *all conversations are with yourself, and sometimes they involve other people. Remember this?* I may think I see you as you are, but in truth, I see you as *I am.* I see you through my own highly individualized context. The implications are staggering, and not the least of them is this: *The issues in my life are rarely about you. They are almost always about me.* This means that I cannot come out from behind myself into conversations with others and make them real until I know who *I am* and what I intend to do with my life.

Whether you end up spending several hours at home or manage to get away for a day or two, your work, your relationships, and your life will begin to be transformed by addressing these questions. We bring into our lives whatever we have the most clarity about. The trouble is, most of us have a great deal of clarity about what we *don't* want. So guess what we get!

Clarify what you want and don't allow your inner critic to edit your answers to the following questions. Set reality considerations aside. Just write whatever comes to mind. If you hear yourself answering "I don't know" to any of the questions, ask yourself, "What would it be if I *did* know?"

Your stump speech will include relationships when you get to "Who is going with me?" but it is not focused on relationships. It is about *your* life. It's the bigger picture into which your relationships will fit. It should give you goose bumps. If it doesn't, you aren't there yet.

My stump speech has changed over the years. Most of us have to live a little before we realize what's most important to us. Your stump speech will be entirely different than mine because no one in the world can do a better job of being you than you.

I quoted Annie Dillard in chapter 6: "How we spend our days is how we spend our lives." How do you want to spend your days, your life? What do you want the next phase of your life to be about? Imagine yourself in full bloom.

> "Who am I and who do I wish to become?"

Having answered the question "Who am I and who do I wish to become?" we are led closer to effectiveness, happiness, satisfaction, calmness, and quietude. Our results are not out there somewhere. We *are* our results, so we must get it right from the core out! We don't automatically self-combust. We must continually and intentionally set ourselves on fire.

I've edited my stump speech several times over the last twenty years. If it will be of help to you, here is my latest version.

Susan's Stump Speech

WHERE AM I GOING?

I am dedicated to fostering human connection—at a deep level—with all people, including those of differing ethnicities, socioeconomic backgrounds, and life experience, and in so doing, to deepen our understanding that what matters anywhere, matters everywhere.

WHY AM I GOING THERE?

I am not neutral. I believe that our conversations will succeed or fail to the degree that we ...

... understand that there is more than one right way to live a life.

... gain the capacity and commitment to connect with, understand, and respect those whose perspectives differ from ours.

... replace the desire to be right with the desire to get it right.

... recognize that while no single conversation is guaranteed to change the trajectory of our civilization, any single conversation can.

WHO IS GOING WITH ME?

Those who have the courage to live lives of ever-deepening authenticity and have passion for their work, the desire to continually learn and improve, and the grace that comes from ongoing personal transformation. Those who put the greater good ahead of narrow self-interest and whose egos are checked at the door.

HOW AM I GOING TO GET THERE?

I will get there by ...

... practicing human connection in each moment, with the person across the table in the meeting, the one holding forth or sitting quietly, the one cooking dinner, the one with whom I disagree, the one I haven't valued and haven't really seen. Until now.

... by choosing the road less taken, again and again.

· ... by being kind because everyone is carrying a heavy load.

... by remembering that I am the one who needs this the most.

Your turn. Grab a piece of paper and figure out what your personal stump speech will be. Revisit it from time to time, perhaps as each year comes to a close. Ask yourself if anything has changed, if you have more clarity, if there are more powerful words, more precise words you can use.

This has been a conversation with yourself that you will share with your partner, with friends and family. And, of course, this is a wonderful opportunity to ask your partner how he or she would answer these questions, a gentle questioning because of your genuine interest, your desire to understand so that you can support your partner going forward.

This chapter and all subsequent chapters conclude with a model for the conversation I would like you to have with a partner. I offer words you can use and expect that you will use whatever words feel right to you. This is your time to prepare and to actually have the conversation. Schedule some time with your partner—focused time when you aren't distracted by kids or dinner or someone who needs to be somewhere in twenty minutes.

 The Conversation: Do I Want This Relationship?

The ideal outcome of this conversation is to clarify what matters most to you and to your partner at this moment in time so that you have (1) a deeper understanding, (2) a deeper connection, (3) an assurance that your goals and values are aligned, and (4) knowledge of how best to support each other. If you aren't aligned, you have things to think about, talk about further, and course correct if possible.

What you might say:

I would like your feedback on something I've been thinking about. I came across four questions designed to help people clarify what matters most to them. I've written my answers to those questions, and I want to know if my answers seem authentic to you. Are they clear? Am I living up to what I've written? Do you see a change or shift I need to make? You up for that?

Assuming you get a yes, share your stump speech.
This can and should be a rich conversation. Hopefully your

partner will ask questions that will provoke deeper thinking. If your partner doesn't think the answers seem authentic or if he/she feels that you aren't living up to what you've written and need to make changes, don't get defensive! Respond with, "Please say more" or "How could I say it so that it's closer to what you feel is true for me?" or "Where do you think I'm off track?"

If your partner is surprised or seems disturbed by your answers, ask questions. "You seem surprised. Does something I've said cause concern for you?" Your partner's answers to these questions are important. Pay attention.

This is also an opportunity to ask your partner for specific support that would be helpful to you. Examples:

> "Since it's important to me to contribute to our community, would you support me in dedicating one weekend each month to doing something for others?"

> "I want to write that novel I've been thinking about for years, and I'll need to dedicate time to do that. How would you feel if I create a place for writing and hang a Do Not Disturb sign on the door when I'm in writing mode?"

As the conversation winds down, you could say, "I'd like to know how you would answer these questions for yourself. Maybe you could tell me sometime this weekend."

This gives your partner time to think about his/her answers. Hopefully you will gladly support each other going forward, but if you learn that the paths you and your partner are traveling will collide or diverge to the point that continuing together doesn't make sense, it's better to know it now rather than down the road.

Answering the questions posed in this chapter requires time, a pretty deep dive, and honesty. Well done.

12

Conversation 2: Clarifying Conditions—Yours, Mine, Ours

There are two primary choices in life: to accept conditions as
they exist, or accept the responsibility for changing them.
—DENIS WAITLEY

Your significant other is sacred, an equal, and worthy of
love, but if he or she wants to be with you, there are conditions.

Characteristics, attitudes, and behaviors that may have been overlooked
in the first flush of love might become irritating over the years. I think of
The War of the Roses, a movie about a married couple trying everything to get
each other to leave the house in a vicious divorce battle. At one point Barbara
tells her husband, Oliver, that she can't stand the sound he makes when he
chews. It's a dark comedy but things like
that can get to us over time. For example,
would you want to share a lifetime of
meals with someone who chews with their
mouth open, makes loud smacking noises,
or talks with a mouth full of food? This

"What conditions are
essential for both of us to
remain happy and committed
in this relationship?"

may seem trivial, but it would gross me out, which wouldn't bode well for mealtime.

Don't worry, this conversation isn't going to be overly picky. It is, however, going to ask, "What conditions are essential for both of us to remain happy and committed in this relationship?"

PRIMED FOR PROBLEMS

Sometimes—*this is important*—it's someone's attitude that makes a relationship intolerable. Think about the people whose company you enjoy the most. How would you describe their attitude toward life, toward the work that they do, toward what's happening in the world and their role in it? Toward you? Are they interesting or boring? Optimistic or pessimistic?

It would be helpful if people wore a badge on their lapel: "Contains inappropriate language and violent outbursts." "Intended only for immature audiences." "Fluent in creative curses." "Completely self-absorbed." "Not suitable for human consumption." "Entrenched victim."

I want to talk briefly about the last one because, unfortunately, it is fairly prevalent and leads to the end of many relationships. PTSD is very real. There are men and women who have undergone something truly horrific, damaging. That's not what I'm talking about here. When I use the term *entrenched victim*, I'm talking about people who seem to attract trouble and who, therefore, are chronically in need of rescuing, of sympathy.

Bad things keep happening to them and it's never their fault. *He did it to me. She did it to me. They, that, it did it to me.* They see themselves as jellyfish at the whim of the waves. Their lives are just one hot mess after another, they don't recover, and they love to revisit those events and tell you about them with all the gory details. I have a friend who still sees the world in terms of what her former spouse would and would not forgive her for. They divorced twenty years ago.

And then another bad thing happens. And another. And they want to hear you say, "Oh, you poor thing, how awful. Let me help. You're safe with me. I'm here for you whatever you need."

You hope they will begin to see that their life can be fulfilling, that there are changes they could make to lessen the likelihood of so many bad things happening to them. You hope they will stand up straighter. And they don't. Stuff keeps happening to them and they continue to lean on you.

Bad things happen to all of us, and most of us, with any luck, move on and try not to repeat the mistakes that contributed to the bad things.

I'm with Maureen Dowd, an American columnist for the *New York Times*, who wrote: "Woe-is-me is not an attractive narrative." Keep an eye out for this one because, if you miss it, at some point it will dawn on you that even though this person is beautiful, lovable, and worthy, he or she is a magnet for trouble, you have become an enabler, the trouble begets more trouble, and you have compassion fatigue.

Any person who prefers misery to pleasure should go follow their misery and free us from the burden of their presence. We may need to say something that seems harsh, but that will help both of us move on. For example:

I have done all I know how to do to prop you up so that you can function in a healthy way, so that you can recognize how capable and wonderful you are, so that you can live a happy life. Yet you continue to think of yourself, to present yourself as fragile, in need of rescuing and protecting from all the bad things that happen to you. Meanwhile, you fail to recognize that the series of catastrophes in your life are not a result of bad luck. They are a result of bad choices. Your choices. I don't believe this will change unless I step away so that you'll be required to stand on your own two feet. I know you are able to make better choices, fix what's broken, and change what isn't working.

Then step away and plug your ears so that you can resist the continued pleas for help. When you recognize that he or she is not your problem to solve, you will feel lighter and your partner will have an opportunity to engage in some serious introspection, to grow and learn.

If, like me, you are attracted to those who take responsibility for the results in their lives, an entrenched victim would be an unacceptable condition.

Moving on. . . . The question is, What would be deal breakers in your relationship? Related to that, Does your partner know how you feel?

What are your partner's deal breakers? Do you know the answer? Your conversation can be as simple as "I want to understand *your* conditions. Here are mine."

Maybe that doesn't sound simple and you fear it will damage the relationship, but truly, this is not the uncomfortable conversation you might imagine. In fact, this is almost always a conversation that brings couples closer. Why? Because we come to know each other better. Our understanding is deepened. Our values and goals are aligned.

Worst case, this conversation makes visible and audible something you were pretending not to know, and now you have things to think about, talk about further, and course correct if possible.

Remember, *what* we talk about in a relationship and *how* we talk about it determines whether our relationship will thrive, flatline, or fail.

Clarifying and sharing your conditions is one of the most energizing conversations you'll ever have. Remember the conversation I had with Lori and Roger? There are values that matter deeply to us, and it's never a good moment when we realize that our conversations are visits to competing ethical systems.

Beyond core values, what else is important to you? Some things we hunger for are nonnegotiable. Never let yourself get used to missing someone, missing being close, held, hugged, kissed, loved. It numbs your soul, which numbs you to so much more.

Many couples don't touch anymore, don't make love in the traditional sense. They don't talk about it. It has become an indiscussable topic and so, although a conversation about conditions will ideally take place before you commit to someone, it's never too late to have it. You'll share your conditions with your partner, and when it's his or her turn, you'll ask questions and listen like your life depends on it. It kinda does.

TOPICS FOR REVEALING CONVERSATIONS

No one is perfect and we all deserve forgiveness from time to time. Your partner's abysmal sock management skills for example. Annoying but hardly a deal breaker—nor is your partner being fifteen minutes late. But being an hour late, consistently? A compulsive punctual like me would have a hard time with that.

Here are topics that can help you and a potential partner discover what you can forgive, overlook, and live with and what are likely deal break-ers. Take this conversation slowly. You'll know when the answers to these questions deserve further exploration. These are questions that can provoke deeper clarity and understanding.

Don't ask all of these questions in one conversation. That would feel like an interrogation! Work them into your conversations over time.

- On a scale of 1–10, how happy are you most of the time? If you're not happy, why not? Is your life working for you? If not, why not? What is essential to your happiness? What could prevent or has prevented or lessened your happiness?
- What are your core values? How do you define integrity? Tell me about a time when you recognized that you were out of integrity. What did you do?
- What do you want for yourself, for a (or our) relationship? (Children, career, goals, spirituality, money, physical fitness, sex, who does the cooking and cleaning, travel, ideal future? Of particular interest here is whether he or she views you as an equal.)
- What do you see as the differences in our personalities? What's good about these differences? Could any of these cause a problem down the road? Do you feel it's workable for people who are very different to be together?
- Where are we similar? Are we both givers, takers, spenders, savers, athletic, not athletic, love sports, don't love sports, love sex, or could do without it? What's good about our similarities? Could any of our dissimilarities cause a problem?
- What is your primary love language? ("Do unto others" isn't always a good thing.)
- What are your conditions for remaining in a relationship (e.g., monog-amy, truth, growth, integrity, kindness, generosity, happy in his or her own skin, must love dogs, etc.)?
- How will decisions be made? What if we disagree?

- On what topics might we compromise?
- How will money be handled? Yours, mine, ours?
- What are you committed to? (Animal rescue, supporting the arts, ending poverty? A man I met at a party seemed to be committed to loathing. He was a blunt instrument. I couldn't get away from him fast enough.)

Here's a question for you to ask yourself: Who might this person help me become? Who might I help this person become? And because we tend to get so excited about the possibilities, we often overlook the question, Does my partner want to mold me into someone I don't want to be? Am I making the same mistake with him/her? Many a relationship has ended up on the rocks because we didn't ask someone where they were headed in their lives or if they were content not to change in any way.

In chapter 7, you began a list of conditions. What would you add?

The Conversation: Clarifying Conditions

It's important to slow this conversation down so it can find out what it wants and needs to be about. If you aren't clear what your partner means (after all, words mean very different things to different people), ask for clarification.

What I find myself saying in so many conversations is "Say more about that." "What does independence, success, spirituality, passion, career success, [fill in the blank] mean to you?"

What you might say:

I want us to create something beautiful and extraordinary together, so it always gets my attention when I hear about a couple parting, because one or both of them were doing something that was intolerable to the other. Sometimes it's not even something someone did, but rather an attitude or a strongly held belief.

It seems that love isn't truly unconditional, so I've thought about the conditions that, for me, are essential for our relationship to thrive. I'd like to share them with you and get your feedback. Please ask questions if something I say isn't clear and also if you foresee a problem.

Here are mine . . .

What are yours?

If you discover that your partner's conditions conflict with yours or you sense your partner isn't willing to respect your conditions or you are struggling with his or her conditions, don't start a fight! Just listen and take time to process.

You might say:

Are you noticing that some of our conditions might be hard to fulfill? For example . . . I think it's important for both of us to give this some thought. Why don't we do that and circle back with each other this weekend (or tomorrow or whenever makes sense). My hope is that we can resolve any difficulties because the conditions we've shared matter a great deal. Okay?

One of the things I love about this conversation is that in preparing for it, you will become even more clear about what matters most to you. You'll be ready for fierce love when you have a sense that there is more inside you than what you have allowed yourself to express, when you are willing to step out of your safety zone, to step out of yourself into a larger identity. Perhaps what you understood, what you believed when your relationship began, has expanded.

13

Conversation 3: How Are We Really?

Never underestimate the power you have to take your life in a new direction.

—GERMANY KENT

Although the divorce rate in the United States has declined over the last twenty years, roughly 44 percent of marriages still end in divorce. And we do no better the second time around; divorce rates are actually higher with each subsequent marriage. *It appears we didn't learn what we needed to learn the first time.* The average duration of a first marriage in the United States is only eight years. For some of you this will be old news because you're part of that statistic.

I was surprised to learn that in some societies a divorce is no big deal and easy to obtain. In 2019, Luxembourg had a divorce rate of 87 percent. Yowza! In Australia's traditional Aboriginal culture, a woman who wishes to get a divorce may instantly end her existing marriage by saying "I do" to another man. In Samoa, a woman has the right to divorce her husband if he forgets about her birthday, and in Saudi Arabia, husbands who fail to bring coffee to their wives might be at risk of divorce. Those poor husbands must feel like they are walking on glass.

Diving deeper into the statistics, what struck me is that around the world 44 percent of divorces are because of "incompatibilities," which is defined by *Merriam-Webster's Dictionary* as "mutually antagonistic things or qualities." An article in *Divorce Magazine* suggests that "no two people are the same. Every single person has different emotional and physical wants and needs, not to mention personality types." In relationships these differences stand out because partners are often together, even more so in a marriage.

Every couple has incompatibilities. Usually spouses can ignore differences or set them aside to some degree to achieve a harmonious living situation, but it is important that couples don't let those incompatibilities become deal breakers. An article from *Psychology Today* says that "continual compromise" is often used to maintain a relationship's harmony. Couples may break up due to one or both of the partners losing their ability to tolerate their incompatibilities. One or both partners no longer want to compromise.

We all recognize that couples can grow apart, but in a recent study in Australia, the issues that contributed the most to divorce were communication problems and loss of connection.

Can I just say, *I told you*!

To those reading this book, divorce is the last thing you'd ever want, and this chapter will help you and your partner stay current with each other. So if there is an incompatibility growing in seriousness, if there is a loss of connection, a failure of communication, you will recognize it, name it, and find a way to resolve it that doesn't end in goodbye.

I was interested to learn that if you're a woman, you're the one most likely to pull the plug on your marriage. Only 31 percent of divorces are initiated by the husband. One of those was my neighbor.

SHE NEVER SAW IT COMING

On a beautiful Friday morning in July, my neighbor left his wife of thirty-nine years while she was out of town. A moving van loaded furniture from the guest bedroom, his home office, and the family room, plus assorted dishes, pots and pans, and three small potted plants. He called to tell me he was leaving and broke down.

"She'll be mad about the plants," he said as we stood in their garage minutes later. "She'll say they were her favorites, but I just want something alive in my apartment."

When his wife came home to glaring gaps in her décor and a note on the stairs, she didn't notice three missing plants. She noticed the empty spot where her husband had been and knew that if he wouldn't return, her life would never be the same.

A week later he confessed the affair to me, describing his lover as fat, frumpy, and frugal. He wasn't even sure they'd stay together. He was sure only that he wanted a different life, a different wife. Frankly, he confessed, almost anyone new would have done. He just wanted to start over.

His wife, one of the more intelligent and insightful people I know, said, "I didn't see it coming. We didn't fight about anything." When her husband's face would turn blank, she attributed it to the demands of his job. Yet for several months she had been waking in the night, a feeling in her gut, a heaviness on her chest, that something was not right.

Lillian Hellman wrote, "People change and forget to tell each other." The idea of "me," of "you," is not static. We are all changing all the time, and though the "I am changing" conversation may be frightening to contemplate, it is essential. My neighbor hadn't had the courage to tell his wife that he was thinking of leaving, that he wanted a different life.

The prospect of that conversation was too daunting.

SUCCESSIVE METAMORPHOSES

As it happens, I am writing this during the COVID-19 pandemic. Reality changed for all of us, everywhere, in a heartbeat. Everyone made changes because we *had* to make them.

Permit me a small rant. I am sick of commercials for Plexaderm, CarShield, and LeafGuard. Those companies must have made a huge buy because their commercials are incessant. And because of all that we have been through, I am sick of the word *unprecedented*. The use of the word *unprecedented* is unprecedented. Make it stop.

During a crisis such as the pandemic—requiring forced togetherness—relationships accelerated. Whatever was good was amplified. Some couples enjoyed this time together. They cooked together, binge-watched shows, had long talks about what they wanted for the future, made babies. Some couples were stressed. Way too much togetherness. Problems that they had ignored were hard to continue ignoring. They bickered and tried to avoid each other, which was hard to do when they were literally tripping over each other.

The thing is, the problems that surfaced for couples during the pandemic had been present before the pandemic. They just hadn't acknowledged them.

Remember Tom and Louise, the couple whose story set this book in motion? (Louise threw their wedding rings in the lake after Tom said he'd rather be golfing.) One day Tom was going about his life, secure in the illusion that he had arrived at the exact point for which he'd been aiming. The next day he found himself amid the broken, disordered wreckage of a marriage. At some level he had known this was possible, but that was the level at which he applied it to other couples and not to his own marriage.

Tom's lack of awareness wasn't because he was a bad guy. The responsibility for this was on Louise. She hadn't told him that she was pulling away. They hadn't addressed the real issues, hadn't come to terms with reality, hadn't stated their needs. One missing conversation at a time, they moved further and further apart. In the end, there were so many things they needed to talk about, the wheels came off the cart.

WHAT THE PEOPLE OF PAPUA
NEW GUINEA GOT RIGHT

One of the languages in Papua New Guinea has the word *mokita*, which is translated as "that which everyone knows and no one speaks of." The people judge the health of any community by the number of mokitas in it. Your relationship with the one you love is a community of two. What do both of you know but not talk about? Finances? Your sex life? A drinking problem? An unhealthy lifestyle?

There is no loss of integrity in desiring a life that better fits us. We lose integrity when we forget to tell others what we are thinking and feeling, when we fold our tent and steal away in the night.

How did you get to a joyful or difficult place with your partner? You talked yourself there, and if you want, you can talk yourself to somewhere better. So if you are contemplating a change in lifestyle, career, geography, or your relationship, don't fold your tent. Instead, build a campfire. Sit beside the one you care for and begin a conversation during which you are completely truthful.

Granted, being truthful with our partners often feels difficult and even scary. We've tried it and paid the price. But the cost of not telling the truth, especially to the one with whom we share our life, is far greater than telling it and risking the consequences. It's *how* we tell the truth that makes the difference, so let's focus on doing it in a way that will enrich the relationship and deepen love rather than stall or diminish it.

The primary requirement to telling the truth is to describe reality from your perspective without laying blame.

The key to this conversation is "without laying blame." Can you get through an entire week without saying anything critical to your partner, without pointing the finger at him or her?

It takes courage to interrogate multiple, possibly competing, realities. To explain what I mean, it might help to picture your family as a beach ball with different, colored stripes. Each of your family members is standing on a different stripe and is experiencing the family from that perspective. We all know that the oldest child has a different experience than the middle or youngest child. Whose description of what it was like growing up in your family is the right description? Well, each of us owns a piece of the

> Describe reality from your perspective without laying blame.

truth about that. If you're operating from the red stripe and your partner is operating from the blue stripe, you can't even see each other from where you stand.

If I believe that my relationship with my partner is pretty perfect and the few problems we have are the fault of my partner (which I hope he/she will correct), that is my view of the relationship. But what if my partner believes our relationship is rocky and that the problems we have are because of me? How do we work through these two different beliefs and experiences? By telling each other what we are thinking and feeling and removing blame from our conversations. When we remove blame, no one shuts down and we create possibilities that did not exist for us before.

There will be circumstances when you will want to give your partner feedback about something that concerns you. In a later chapter I will show you how to do that in a way that deepens your relationship. In the meantime, removing blame from your conversations can be challenging, so try it out for a day or two or three.

Before you engage your partner in a "How are we really?" conversation, take a look at the following list. Some items will be familiar to you, but they are worth repeating.

SEVEN KEYS TO A SUCCESSFUL "HOW ARE WE REALLY?" CONVERSATION

1: Master the courage to interrogate reality.

No plan survives its collision with reality—and reality has a habit of changing, seriously complicating our plans. Not only do we neglect to share our changing reality with others, but we are skilled at masking it from ourselves. Are you certain that you know what is on your partner's mind? Do you know how your partner feels about your relationship? While you may not like reality, you cannot successfully argue with it. Reality generally wins, whether it's a spouse's changing needs or your own physical or emotional well-being.

2: Come out from behind yourself into the conversation, and make it real.

A careful conversation is a failed conversation because it merely postpones the conversation that wants and needs to take place. While many fear facing reality, it is the unreal conversations that should concern you, because they are incredibly expensive for you and for your relationship. Remove the mask of Perfect Spouse or Happy Family, take a deep breath, and show up honestly. What are the real issues? Name them and speak toward them with firmness and concentration. No one has to change, but everyone has to have the conversation. When the conversation is real, the change can occur before the conversation has ended.

3: Be here, prepared to be nowhere else.

Even if you have a long string of failed conversations with your partner, come into this one with openness and the purity of your attention. In *Tapestry of Fortunes*, Elizabeth Berg wrote: "It is also our tradition to pass on some words of wisdom about how to have a happy marriage. I know a lot of people say things like 'Don't go to bed angry,' 'Start and end each day with a kiss,' 'Be together but also spend some time apart,' that sort of thing. For me, I guess it can all be summed up this way: pay attention. The rest falls into place with that, I think." Unplug the phone, turn off the television, allow ample time. Focus not only on being clear yourself but on understanding your partner.

4: Take responsibility for your emotional wake.

There is no trivial comment. You cannot take back hurtful words delivered carelessly. To ensure that your conversation ends with an afterglow versus an aftermath or aftertaste, do your best to describe reality without laying blame. Deliver your message without creating a hurtful emotional wake by speaking directly to the heart of the issue with clarity, conviction, and compassion.

5: Let silence do the heavy lifting.

Insight occurs in the space between words. The more emotionally loaded a subject, the more silence is required. When you sit quietly with your partner, whatever is in the way—anger, numbness, impatience, manipulation, rigidity, blame, ego, cruelty, ambition, insensitivity, intimidation, pride—may fall away. In silence such attributes, emotions, and behaviors reveal themselves as unnecessary.

Insight occurs in the space between words.

6: Extend a compelling invitation.

Once you've mustered the courage and taken a very deep breath, you might begin the conversation like this: "I know I told you I wanted to be a lawyer, and I'm on track to become a partner, but lately I dream of raising basil, manufacturing pesto. That terrific recipe we created . . ."

Or like this: "I want to talk with you about current reality. Mine, yours, ours. I'm beginning to imagine a different life, to desire significant changes."

7. Have the conversation!

Don't wait for the right time or mood, or you may never have the conversation that could alter everything. Instead of continuing to limp, it's time to remove the stone from your shoe. Your partner may be expecting this conversation and will ultimately be relieved that you are talking.

Something within us responds to those who level with us. My friend George had a sense that when his wife said, "I love you," it was a question rather than a statement. He shared this with her and the conversation that followed was one of the most meaningful they'd had in a very long time.

 ## The Conversation: How Are We Really?

Before I provide questions for you and your partner to explore, here's a conversational model you can use to interrogate reality on any topic with your partner and with others. We will put it to work in a later chapter.

Conversational Model

Step 1: Name the topic you want to discuss.

If it's a problem, what is at the core of the problem? If you can't name it, you can't solve it. Be clear and concise. Perhaps you're thinking of changing careers or you'd like to move from the city to the country or you want to make a significant shift in lifestyle. Obviously all of these things would involve and impact your partner, so don't keep your thoughts to yourself. Put them out there for discussion. Here is the flow:

I've been thinking about . . .
It's important to me because . . .
Here are the options I've been considering . . .
If I had to make a decision or take action today without your
  input, I'd choose . . .

You are acknowledging your reality and giving your partner an opportunity to learn more about how you see things.

Step 2: Invite your partner's perspective.
Now it's important to invite your partner to weigh in and to influence your thinking: "I believe this would be a good thing, a good course of action. But you may see it differently. What are your thoughts? Feel free to challenge my thinking."

This takes courage. You might discover that your partner doesn't see things the way you do. *At all!* You could have your opinions, attitudes, and beliefs challenged. You might discover that your partner would vehemently object to the plan of action you are considering and, in fact, has been thinking of some changes that would substantially conflict with what *you* had in mind. *Or* you could learn that your partner agrees with you, has been thinking along the same lines. Or somewhere in between.

NOTE: Let your partner *actually* push back. Resist the temptation to defend yourself or strengthen your own case. Say "Tell me more. Help me understand your thinking." And mean it.

Questions to Discuss with Your Partner

It's important to embrace the fact that you and your partner will not agree on everything. During forty-plus years of research on happily married couples, clinical psychologist John Gottman discovered that the happiest couples have persistent unresolved conflicts. He points out that the idea that couples must resolve all their problems is a fairy tale.

Still, even when resolution is unlikely, clarity is essential. When you and your partner answer the questions below, no matter how close you are, you will likely learn things you didn't know, which is a great way to enrich the relationship.

The first nine questions are about you as individuals. Having written and shared your stump speech, the answers to these questions may not be a surprise. Discussing these will prime the pump for delving into the next five questions, which are about your relationship.

Answer each question for yourself, share your answer with your partner, then ask your partner the same question. This needn't be a marathon. If a question leads to a long conversation, stop there. Take another question on another day.

What you might say:

We can make our journey together ordinary and boring or joyful and uplifting. I vote for the latter, so I think we should check in with each other from time to time in case anything has changed or any new thoughts or goals have emerged. I want to be the best partner possible for you, and there are questions we could explore that will help us know how to best support and encourage each other. Plus, there is always more to learn about each other.

1. What one experience do I most want to have in my life? What have I allowed to be in the way? What step could I take to move in that direction?
2. What do I most want to accomplish in my life? What could I do to advance this goal?
3. What activity have I always dreamed of doing that I haven't yet done?

4. If I could be mentored by anyone, living or dead, whom would I select as my mentor? Why? What would I hope to learn?

5. What trait do I most deplore in myself? In others?

6. What is my greatest fear?

7. On what occasions do I lie?

8. What one or two words describe me best?

9. What is my motto?

10. What is the quality I value most in a partner, in you?

11. Is there a recent conversation where either of us felt we were avoiding the real issue? If not, hooray for us! If yes, what is the issue we avoided? Let's talk about it now.

12. How are we doing financially, given our long-term goals? Do we need to make any changes, adjustments? Are there steps we need to take?

13. If we were guaranteed honest responses from each other to any three questions, here's what I would ask. (Ask them.)

14. What one thing could I do, you do, we do that would enrich our relationship?

NOTE: Question 13 can be tricky. Don't ask a question if you are not ready to hear an honest answer. For example, don't ask, "What one thing would you like to change about me?" unless you are prepared to hear "I'd like you to lose weight." Or "I wish you were more enthusiastic in bed." That's a good question and there is value in knowing how your partner would answer it, even if you don't want to hear it, but you get to decide what you're up for.

Don't ask, "Have you ever been attracted to anyone else since we've been together?" We've all been attracted to others during an exclusive relationship. That's not the same as taking action on that attraction. On the other hand, if you have reason to suspect an affair, that's a tough conversation to navigate successfully, so I'll tell you how to approach that conversation later.

Be truthful and encourage your partner to be truthful. Along the way both of you will gain the understanding, respect, patience, forgiveness, and support that are essential to a healthy and happy relationship.

14

Conversation 4: Getting Past "Honey, I'm Home"

When someone receives us with open-hearted, non-judging,
intensely interested listening, our spirits expand.
—SUE THOELE

Speaking purely for myself, if you and I were to meet, I wouldn't be particularly interested in what school you went to, how much money you make, or your score on the last nine holes. Many conversations consist of "How are you?" "Fine, how are you?" "Looks like rain again today." "Yep." Exchanges like this remind me of a cartoon I saw years ago. A woman holding a bowl leans toward a dog. The dog is jumping. The caption: "Oh boy! Dog food again!"

If you are going to be an important person in my life, I would want to get past "How are you?" "I'm fine." Way past. I would want to know what makes you happy, what makes you sad, angry. I would want to know what you long for, what you most hope to accomplish during your lifetime, who and what you love, how you would describe your ideal day, what you would wish for if a genie popped out of a bottle. (I'd wish that I could be fluent in every language on the planet.) The kinds of things that, if you've been having the conversations in previous chapters, have probably revealed themselves.

I would want to know if you've paid the price for transparency, if you're willing to live, day by day, with the consequences of authenticity. Or if you withhold your thoughts and feelings for fear of being abandoned. And from a poem by Ron Koertge with the marvelous title "Admission Requirements of U.S. and Canadian Dental Schools": "If you were a bird, what would be your wingspan?" And "If you could snow, would you?"

How I wish people would ask me questions like that.

I would definitely, enthusiastically snow, gently, quietly, persistently, enticing children to come out and play. I'd be a winter wren the size of a demitasse, and although my wingspan would be small, my song would be operatic. Or perhaps I'd be a golden eagle with a nest high in a pine tree in the Scottish Highlands. The possibilities are wonderful.

We asked many questions in the first blush of love, but now we meet up at the end of the day, having tackled our to-do list and encountered challenges along the way, and those things are mentioned only in passing, if at all.

"More crap from Dave about why he keeps missing deadlines."

"There's some pretty toxic gossip going on in the office."

"Sometimes I think I should look for a different job."

Or you see that faraway look that tells you your partner has something on his or her mind, but neither of you go there. There's dinner to cook, kids' homework to inspect, the dog is desperate for a walk.

That's okay. Sometimes. But if you pick up that your partner is dealing with a problem (he or she might come right out and tell you), you have an opportunity to connect with your partner at that deep level I keep going on about. Maybe not this exact minute. Gotta feed the kids. But later, after dinner, before you both go to sleep.

The conversation that achieves intimacy and connection better and quicker than any other is the conversation you'll learn in this chapter. I think of it as my Swiss Army Knife conversation because I've used it with family, friends, and executives and their teams, as well as strangers on airplanes. I can't tell you how many times a stranger has said, midconversation, "I can't believe I'm telling you this!" Sometimes my thought is, *I can't believe you're telling me this either, but keep going because this is better than anything on TV!* It's a going-deeper conversation, getting past "Honey, I'm home."

It's powerful. You will connect with your partner by creating a container of safety and intimacy in which the most important things will surface.

This conversation is about your *partner*, not you or your relationship. It is especially helpful when your partner has something weighing on his or her mind, something he or she is wrestling with. You will ask questions and say very little. You'll help your partner think out loud by talking candidly about what he or she is dealing with and what he or she needs to do about it. Some possible topics are:

- A situation at work.
- A relationship with a coworker, friend, or relative.
- A health concern or frustration.
- Something that needs doing that he or she is avoiding.
- General satisfaction with the career path (or life path) he or she is on.
- A tough decision he or she needs to make.

It could be anything, really. One of the most valuable and truly magical things about this conversation is that you will help your partner identify the *real* issue, the one that's causing the symptoms. You know that your partner hasn't identified it yet, or has identified it but has avoided tackling it, because your partner is still complaining about the same thing he or she complains about all the time.

Continuing to dance around the issue isn't helpful. What's at the center? The source? What's the most important thing that needs tackling?

> Continuing to dance around the issue isn't helpful.

For example, if you've read *Beowulf,* then you know that while Grendel was a terror, his mother was far worse. Here's the short version:

In Denmark there lived King Hrothgar, beloved by his men, who enjoyed evenings at the mead hall drinking, telling stories, singing songs. One night the door burst open and a ferocious creature called Grendel burst into the room and dismembered several men before dragging one of them, screaming, out into the night. They had heard about Grendel but thought he might be just a myth. Clearly, he was real. This put quite a damper on the party, but it was a real high for Grendel, who returned the very next night. Though the men were armed and ready, they couldn't defeat him. More carnage.

Lucky for Hrothgar, Beowulf, a traveling hero-for-hire, showed up the next day looking for work. Hrothgar offered Beowulf anything he wanted if he would slay Grendel. After hearing how many men Grendel had killed, Beowulf was a little worried, but in true hero fashion, decided to give it a go.

When Grendel returned for his third deadly raid on the mead hall, the horrific battle was on. Beowulf barely survived but finally managed to tear off one of Grendel's arms and the creature fled into the night, howling and bleeding profusely from his fatal wound.

Everyone celebrated, Beowulf was rewarded many treasures and the parties resumed.

Imagine everyone's horror when a few nights later, in the darkest hour, the door to the mead hall came off its hinges and filling the doorway was Grendel's mother. She was far bigger and badder than Grendel and she was *mad*. Many more men died that night.

Clearly Beowulf's job wasn't over, so he headed out to the grassy marshes and boggy swamps where Grendel's mother lived, finally arriving at a black lake where he watched as wild dogs pursued a stag to the water's edge. Rather than go into the black water, the stag stopped on the edge of the lake and was taken down by the dogs. The problem was, Grendel's mother lived in a cave beneath that lake.

Beowulf had serious misgivings about what was ahead of him, but what's a hero to do? Beowulf removed his heavy armor and swam down, down, down, into the lake, to the cave where he discovered Grendel's mother sleeping. When he raised his sword to kill her, she awoke, his sword disintegrated, and he stood before her with empty hands as she attacked.

Just when he was about to take his last breath, his fingers found the handle of a dagger on the floor of the cave, which he drove into her throat, killing her.

By the way, they made this into a movie with Angelina Jolie as Grendel's mother. (I don't think so!) But here's the lesson for those of us who truly want to be helpful to someone we care for. Are you and your partner dinking around with Grendel, or a series of Grendels, while Grendel's mother is alive and well and about to cause serious damage?

Your goal is to help your partner find out if Grendel has a mother, and it's unlikely that you'll find her on the surface. You'll have to go into the conversational lake, beneath the surface, where few are eager to go. And once you're there, all of the coaching techniques you may have learned will not help you. Best to go in with empty hands and use what you find when you arrive.

HEART + SMART

The questions in this conversation will help your partner not only clarify the issue but also get in touch with emotions. Why does this matter?

Daniel Kahneman, a Princeton psychologist, won the Nobel Prize for his studies by proving we make decisions and act on them first for emotional reasons and second for rational reasons. When we stay in our heads, we can talk about a problem all day and be in no danger of doing anything about it. It's only when some heat—a.k.a. *emotion*—is introduced that we are motivated to act.

The challenge in this conversation is that we are not acquainted with our emotions much of the time. Authentic emotions are hard to identify, and so we satisfy ourselves with conventional sentiments without asking "Is this what I'm really feeling?" This kind of authenticity, this thinking further and putting our finger on what we are truly feeling, is powerful. It's where the magic comes in.

> It's important to ask your partner what he or she is feeling and let silence do the heavy lifting.

For many of us, asking about emotions feels awkward, inappropriate, but it's essential. Emotions give the lit match something to ignite, and because feelings are slower than thoughts, it's important to ask your partner what he or she is feeling and let silence do the heavy lifting. Otherwise your partner may stay in his or her head about the issue and fail to take action. In this conversation your goal is for your partner to identify at least one thing to improve the situation and then do it.

MINERAL RIGHTS

Many years ago an attendee at one of our Fierce workshops named this conversation Mineral Rights because, if you're mining for gold, you will likely be more successful if you dig deep rather than simply rake the ground on the surface. You're more likely to find water if you dig a single one-thousand-foot-deep well than one thousand one-foot-deep wells.

I wrote about the Mineral Rights conversation in my first book, *Fierce Conversations*, and we teach it in our courses. The questions will help your partner think further about the issue than perhaps they have previously, smoke out Grendel's mother if she is lurking nearby, and identify a plan of action, even if it's just one step.

First, let's talk about where we go wrong when we try to be helpful.

ADVICE GIVERS' DILEMMA: THE PERILS OF PROBLEM-SOLVING

There are problems with the curse of expertise. No matter how much you've accomplished, no matter how many times you've solved similar problems, the following are true: (a) you don't have answers for everything because, ahem, you don't know everything; (b) if you provide the answers, your partner doesn't need to think for him/herself; (c) if your advice doesn't work out, you're to blame; (d) like most people, your partner isn't likely to take your advice because he or she values self-generated insight over outside input; and (e) you and your partner may have expended all this time and effort tilting with Grendel while his mother is chortling in the corner, sharpening her nails.

Sadly, when someone says, "I have a problem," we quickly respond with, "I had a similar situation. Here's what I did to solve it . . ." How long was this conversation about your partner before you took it away and made it about you? One minute? Mere seconds?

You may have heard the saying, "If I had an hour to solve a problem, I'd spend fifty-five minutes thinking about the problem and five minutes thinking about solutions." This is good advice. After all, if you told your doctor you had a rash and he or she prescribed an ointment without asking you any questions, you'd think twice about seeing that doctor again. We need to clarify what's actually going on and what could happen if we don't handle it well *before* we land on solutions. That's what you will help your partner do by asking questions and listening deeply to your partner's answers.

THE SECRET RULE

There is a secret rule that you will give yourself. Questions only! No advice! Not a single declarative statement until your partner has answered the last question. Then and *only* then, if you have a suggestion you can offer it, but only one. Or better yet, none. When you are giving advice, you are doing the talking and your partner is listening. We're going to reverse this.

By the way, you can actually ask *yourself* these questions about an issue on your plate, on your mind, on your heart, or you can ask a friend to ask you these questions. I swear by it.

Let's focus your attention on your partner.

The Conversation: Getting Past "Honey, I'm Home" (Your Swiss Army Knife)

There are seven steps to moving beyond a surface-level conversation and finding a deeper connection with your partner. Below I've outlined the questions you need to ask to get from one step to the next.

STEP #1. If your partner tells you about an issue on his or her plate, you have the starting point for this conversation. If not, then ask, "When you think about everything you're dealing with these days, everything that's on your plate, what's the most important thing on your mind?"

If your partner says, "I don't know," ask, "What would it be if you did know? I ask because I truly want to know what you're dealing with these days."

Hopefully, your partner will give it some thought and say something like, "Well, I'm frustrated with a situation at work . . ." You're launched.

STEP #2. Ask questions about the issue: "What's going on relative to _____?" "How long has it been going on?" "Tell me more."

Sometimes it helps to tell your partner what you think you're hearing, for example, "So, the issue is . . ." Don't be surprised if your partner says, "Well, not exactly." This is useful. You're helping her locate Grendel's mother if she's there.

STEP #3. Now it's time to further clarify why this issue is important. "What results is this creating? What else is it affecting? Who is it affecting?" Ask, "What else?" at least three times. Then ask, "How is this currently impacting you?"

This question conveys our care for our partner, our love, and often evokes an emotional response, which is a good thing. Go a bit deeper by asking, "When you consider everything you just described, what do you feel?" (*Note*: Not "How does this make you feel?")

Let's say they respond, "Frustrated!" Say, "Frustrated. Say more about that."

And after they've said more, ask, "What else do you feel?"

STEP #4. This next question will heighten your partner's awareness about what may happen if things stay the same and, consequently, will motivate your partner to take action. "If nothing changes, what are the implications?" You could say, "Imagine it is a year from now and nothing has changed. What is likely to happen?" "What else?" "What's likely to happen for you if nothing changes?" Again, probe for emotion. "When you consider those possible outcomes, what do you feel?"

STEP #5. To help your partner recognize any contributions he or she may have made to the issue, ask: "When I'm faced with a problem, I can usually see my DNA on it somewhere, my contribution to the problem. Do you see your fingerprints anywhere on this issue?"

This is not the time to add your thoughts about where your partner went wrong, so don't comment on your partner's response other than to say, "That's useful to recognize." Move on.

STEP #6. This next question points to the light at the end of this tunnel and propels your partner to take action. Ask, "When this has been resolved and is no longer a problem, what difference will that make?" Ask, "What else?" Then ask, "What difference will that make for you?" And finally, "When you contemplate that scenario, what do you feel?"

STEP #7. So you don't leave your partner full of emotion with no place to go, ask, "What's the next most useful step you can take to begin to resolve this issue?" Again, if your partner says, "I don't know," ask, "What would it be if you did know?" "I don't know" is too easy, too lazy, and rarely true. Help your partner be better, braver, clearer. "What are you committed to do and when?" "What will try to get in your way and how will you get past that?"

Common Mistakes

Doing most of the talking.

> **Partner:** I'm having this problem at work.
> **You:** Oh yeah, I know what you mean. I had that same problem. What happened was . . .

Giving advice.

> **Partner:** My coworker isn't living up to our agreements. I'm doing all the work.
> **You:** You should confront her. You should tell your boss. You should . . .

Not inquiring about emotions.

> **Partner:** I think I'm about to be laid off from my job.
> **You:** Well, that might not be a bad thing. You don't love that job. Maybe it's time to make a change.

Moving too quickly from question to question, which often morphs into accusations.

> **Partner:** You and I haven't had a date night in a year.
> **You:** Well, whose fault is that?
> **Partner:** It's not anybody's fault. I just think . . .
> **You:** Why haven't you suggested it?
> **Partner:** Actually, I did. A couple of times.
> **You:** Did you say it was important, that you were serious?
> **Partner:** I thought I did, but . . .
> **You:** What kind of date? Dinner, movie?
> **Partner:** Maybe a weekend.
> **You:** With our schedules, do you really think that's possible?

Right about this time, your partner would probably look for an exit, because you turned a conversation that could have been loving into a grilling that was not loving, not helpful.

Remember, the conversation *is* the relationship. If your goal is to create a love that lasts, your conversations should be an experience that helps to accomplish that. In this conversation, your job is to slow this conversation down so it can find out what it wants and needs to be about. In the process, your partner will feel heard, understood, loved, and genuinely helped, and your relationship will be enriched.

15

Conversation 5: Let Me Count the Ways

Tell me, tell me, tell me!
—HOLLY HUNTER, *ALWAYS*

Valentine's Day. What to give? Flowers, chocolate? Absolutely, but the best gift I received from a wonderful man in my past was a list of things he loved about me. He read them aloud, then put the list on my refrigerator door so I'd be reminded often. There are fifty-one. They are deeply personal, and he clearly gave it a lot of thought, which is why this meant so much. At the risk of seeming egotistic, I will share a few to give you ideas because I hope you will create a list for the one you love. Don't wait for Valentine's Day.

My list began (in no particular order):

1. You care about people.
2. You laugh and smile a lot.
3. Your face always reveals your mood.
4. You love the outdoors.
5. You go after what it is you want.

6. You have that "tuning fork" quality: calming, reassuring.
7. You are loving and respectful of children.
8. You are one "outta sight" dancer.
9. You are up close and personal, and in my face.
10. You are spontaneous, exciting, and in the present.
11. You give me space and claim your own.
12. You tell me what is going on with you.
13. You are curious, wanting to know more.
14. You're vulnerable and sometimes look like a little girl.
15. Your expressive vocabulary and phrases.
16. Your fingers on my arm.
17. You're always on time.
18. You connected and cared for your father.
19. Your insistence on a cup of coffee first thing in the morning.
20. Your tears are an indicator of what is touching you.

Maybe your list will say, "I love the way you help fix dinner, talk with my mother, think of fun things to do on weekends, read interesting articles to me, ask for my thoughts about your work situation, really listen to me, come up behind me when I'm at the sink and wrap your arms around me, [fill in the blank]." That's fierce. That's real and there aren't nearly enough of those conversations.

Because "Thanks, babe," doesn't cut it. Nor does "Good job." Or even "I appreciate you." Those are vague. What's more meaningful is an affirmation that is specific. Even "I love you" isn't guaranteed to truly mean something to your partner, especially if you say it all the time as a matter of course, such as a shouted, "Love you!" as you head out the door. Not that that's bad. It just isn't enough.

FLATTERY GETS YOU NOWHERE

Frequent, undeserved flattery and praise are suspect. When we lavish it on our children, they may think they are God's gift for simply breathing. When we flatter a woman about her appearance but little else, the message can be that she doesn't have anything else of value to contribute. Much of our flattery and praise is insincere and the recipients know this, but it's habitual, expected, a societal norm.

When we are consistently flattered, it can be damaging because it tamps down our ability to recognize and accept the real thing when it comes along. So let's learn to express our appreciation for someone in a way that they can really hear, feel, and embrace.

When someone who rarely gives me compliments does compliment me, it means more, especially if they say something I don't hear every day.

On the other hand, when someone frequently flatters or praises me, I feel like taking a step back from them. My trust radar kicks in and I wonder what they're after. I flatter you in the hope that by inflating your ego you will like me, value me, promote me, desire me. I don't respond well when someone tries to inflate my ego. It feels insincere and I want to shake it off, walk away, stay away. The state of my ego, which has its ups and downs, is an inside job, so don't try to mess with it. *Thank you.*

> Frequent, undeserved flattery and praise are suspect.

My view about praise and flattery may be controversial, so try an experiment. The next time you meet up with a friend, relative, or coworker, just say hello. Don't add, "You look great" or something like that. I imagine that will feel uncomfortable. Hold your compliment, your praise, your flattery for a genuine, 100 percent certifiably praiseworthy moment. If there isn't one, don't worry. There will be some day, some moment, and then whatever you say will mean something to the recipient because they know you don't throw out praise for no good reason.

THREE MEMORABLE WORDS

A favorite memory occurred decades ago when I was about to lead my first human-potential training. The course was called the Pursuit of Excellence. I had taught high school right out of college and knew I loved to teach because that's when I learn the most myself, but I had not "taught" adults. There had been so much to learn. Three evenings and an entire weekend with up to one thousand people attending. It was exhilarating and terrifying. An enormous facilitator notebook and so many people who had paid for what they hoped would be a life-changing experience.

I had pleaded with the founder to allow me to do this and had finally been given permission. Would I be allowed to lead more sessions after this one? The stakes were high.

My mentor stood in front of me just before the first evening began and looked solemnly into my face. I was ready for the pep talk. Something along the lines of "You'll do great! You know this stuff, so go out there and knock 'em dead!" Instead, he said, "I have just three words for you. And they're important." I could hardly breathe. I stood very still, waiting for three magic words of encouragement and affirmation. He leaned close, looked deep into my eyes, and said, "Don't screw up."

I burst out laughing and walked onto the stage with genuine joy and a huge smile on my face. Perhaps you wouldn't have reacted in the same way, but for me, those words acknowledged that he got me, got my sense of humor, and knew I'd be fine. In the intervening years, I have gifted these three words to our Fierce facilitators when we celebrate their certification. They laugh, as I did, and we're good to go.

THE ONE-MINUTE MANAGER

The premise of Ken Blanchard's book *The One Minute Manager* is that you should catch people in the act of doing something right and comment on it. One minute or less of appreciation. Also, if you notice something that's not great, comment on that in the moment, not waiting for a formal performance review. One minute or less of gentle correction. This is a brilliant little book. Of course, it was quickly followed by *The 59-Second Employee: How to Stay One Second Ahead of Your One-Minute Manager* by Rae André and Peter D. Ward.

I agree wholeheartedly with Blanchard's approach and wrote about it in *Fierce Leadership: A Bold Alternative to the Worst "Best" Practices of Business Today*. Rather than anonymous feedback, which has done so much damage over the years, I want people to stay current with one another by giving feedback 365 days a year—face-to-face, if possible. Feedback isn't positive or negative. Feedback is just feedback, and it can and should include drawing attention to something someone did well.

> Feedback isn't positive or negative. Feedback is just feedback, and it can and should include drawing attention to something someone did well.

I recommend this to you and your partner. If you see your partner do something really well, something for which you are grateful, something that touches you, speak up. One minute or less of recognition. Let this be your default setting, rather than negativity. So let's think about how to do this well.

EVERY WORD THE RIGHT WORD

We are as terrible at giving compliments as we are at receiving them. Even our offhand compliments can be felt as insincere, undeserved, or unclear. "Good job" doesn't tell me much. *What was it that I did in this job that was good? No clue.*

Remember the notion of emotional wake and how we always leave one? Like boats that leave a wake—from big waves that could cause a small boat nearby to capsize, to small ones that get our attention but cause little damage—our wake is the feeling people have after being in our company. "Good job" leaves a feeble wake compared with telling someone, "I overheard you talking with Ellie about what happened at school. It sounded like you were able to calm her down and help her figure out how to handle it. I was impressed by your compassion and how straightforward you were with her, how you helped her see her part in the incident."

WHAT I APPRECIATE ABOUT YOU

We'd like to be appreciated for who we are and what we do, but who is responsible for providing this *appreciation* we all crave so much?

At Fierce we have an exercise that teams do from time to time. We sit in a circle and each person takes their turn in the "warm seat." They have sixty seconds to tell the team what they feel they bring to the team. Then the team members have about five minutes to take turns telling the team member what, exactly, they appreciate about that person. "You do such a good job" doesn't cut it. What, specifically, is it that they do so well? The comments are precise, thoughtful.

It gets very real, very warm, and most importantly, the comments land because they are often about the person's character, how helpful they were on a project, or how much their sense of humor is appreciated. Sometimes there are tears in the eyes of both the person in the warm seat and those who are telling that person what they appreciate about them.

The person in the warm seat can say only one thing after each team member has spoken: "Thank you."

I recommend you do this with your partner. Don't wait for a formal "warm seat" session. Be spontaneous. Catch yourself feeling love or warmth or gratitude or admiration or whatever for your partner and tell them in the moment.

If this all feels a bit uncomfortable, that's because you may not have experienced this growing up. My friend Jose used to tell me how much time he spent with his young daughter, how he constantly told her how wonderful she was because he wanted her to look for that kind of treatment when she looked for a husband someday. He was shocked when a family therapist told him, "Jose, that's not what she will look for. Her model for a husband is not how you treat *her*. It's how you treat her mother. Do you express your love and appreciation for her mother in front of her? Do you spend quality time with her mother? That's what she needs to see."

What a powerful thing to understand. Children watch the relationship between their parents as a model for marriage. If you think back to your childhood, what did your parents model for you? How did that affect you? How did your parents' interactions influence how you interact with a partner? If you have children, what are you modeling for them?

Time for homework.

The Conversation: Let Me Count the Ways

Imagine you come home and your partner is in the kitchen chopping onions. As you enter the kitchen, he pours a glass of wine.

He says, "I thought I'd start prepping for dinner. I know you hate to chop onions. That's your favorite Cab, by the way."

You may be exhausted from all the craziness you had to deal with at work, too tired to muster the level of gratitude this calls for. But muster it anyway. This is an opportunity to be specific in "counting the ways," like the list given to me that was on my refrigerator for a very long time and the exercise teams do in my company. I would like to think you would look at your husband, look at the glass of wine, walk over to him, and say something like:

> You, my husband, are a miracle of manhood! This is so sweet, so thoughtful. Thank you, thank you, thank you. I lift this glass to you.

Or maybe you're both binge-watching something on TV and you realize this is one of those perfect moments. It just comes over you. You might say something like:

> For me this is a perfect moment. I'm cuddled up with the person I love, watching a show we both enjoy in our cozy home, safe—at least temporarily—from the demands of the outside world. I love us. I love you.

Or your partner tells you about helping one of your children deal with a struggle at school. You might say something like:

> That was such good advice. I don't know how you came by your wisdom, but our children are very lucky to be guided by someone as loving and wise as you. You are a spectacular parent.

Sometimes you don't have to say anything. A glance, a smile, a hug, a kiss, a cuddle. The point is, people don't always know how we feel about them unless we tell them, show them. If you wish your partner would be more affectionate, *you* be more affectionate. If you wish your partner would show more gratitude for all that you do, *you* express gratitude for all that your partner does. You go first. Often. Model what you would like to experience. You can even pick up the phone in the middle of the day and call your partner just to tell them you were thinking of them and how much you love them.

Of course, there's always room for humor. When a friend told her husband that she thinks of him when she hears certain music, he said, "I hope it's not the *Jaws* theme. *Da dum. Da dum.*"

16

Conversation 6: It's Not You, It's Me

A genuine apology is like an eleventh-hour rain on a dusty crop.
Grossly overdue, but miraculously just in time.
—JACQUELINE A. BUSSIE

A myth I didn't include in the list of myths that mislead and derail us is the infamous line, "Love means not ever having to say you're sorry," from Erich Segal's novel *Love Story*, which was adapted into a movie starring Ali MacGraw and Ryan O'Neal. The line has been mocked for suggesting that apologies are unnecessary in a loving relationship. Another character played by O'Neal disparages it in the 1972 screwball comedy *What's Up, Doc?* In that film's final scene, Barbra Streisand's character says, "Love means never having to say you're sorry," while batting her eyelashes, and O'Neal's character responds in a deadpan voice, "That's the dumbest thing I ever heard."

And it is.

When someone apologizes, it's amazing how much fresh air enters the room. Sometimes we do and say hurtful things. Thankfully, we cut one another a fair amount of slack day to day. Relationships don't survive unless we are willing to tolerate imperfections in our partners and recognize that we have a few of our own, which we too often fail to acknowledge and apologize for.

> When someone apologizes, it's amazing how much fresh air enters the room.

It is difficult to admit that you are wrong, particularly if you have been wrong for a very long time. And it's hard to admit that you just did or said something that left a negative emotional wake and potentially harmed the relationship.

We often navigate our lives like competent but distracted drivers. We have passed our driving test and accumulated experience on the road. We clutch the steering wheel as we whiz along the road of life, wondering what will appear next, just beyond the reach of our headlights or over the next hill.

So here we are with the skills and knowledge to operate this fast-moving vehicle, but have we created any roadkill along the way?

STRIKING A BALANCE

Before I offer an approach to apologizing, let's acknowledge that we can go too far. You may know someone whose mantra is "I'm sorry." One day, a coworker got to me. Here are snippets of dialogue with her one morning:

> **Me:** I'm having trouble formatting this document.
> **Her:** I'm sorry.
> **I wish she had said:** I'll find someone who can help you with this.

> **Me:** Traffic was horrible today.
> **Her:** I'm sorry.
> **I wish she had said:** I know. It sucks.

> **Me:** Mark is late for our meeting.
> **Her:** I'm sorry.
> **I wish she had said:** I'll track him down.

I thought about throwing her a curve and saying, "Pretty sure I'll live longer than you." Pretty sure she'd say, "I'm sorry."

I finally asked her why she said "I'm sorry" so often. "So far today you've said you're sorry about my formatting issues, you're sorry about the traffic, and you're sorry Mark is late. As if everything is your fault. Can you tell me why you say you're sorry so often?"

She looked confused. "Well, I guess I am sorry you're having a tough time. I empathize."

I replied, "You have a good heart, and if I told you that I was in pain, it would be comforting for you to say that you're sorry I'm in pain. It's just that if you start listening to yourself, you will realize how often you say you're sorry. You didn't write the code for formatting. You don't control Seattle traffic. And you aren't Mark's keeper. Those apologies were unnecessary. I think it's just a habit I hope you will break."

For the next few days, she'd start to say "I'm sorry" and catch herself. I'd give her a thumbs up. Eventually she broke the habit. I think her spine straightened a bit. (Maybe that was my imagination.)

Apologizing too often is irritating and, frankly, kind of pathetic. Never apologizing is worse. When we knowingly lock down words of apology, a little part of us hardens. The more we refuse to apologize when we know we were in the wrong, the stonier we become until we are hard, cold, and alone.

I understand that apologizing doesn't come easy. It takes a big person, so be big.

ARMAND GAMACHE'S ADVICE

I am a fan of Louise Penny's murder mysteries set around the life of Chief Inspector Armand Gamache of the provincial police force for Quebec. An unanticipated benefit within these books has been Inspector Gamache's counsel to those he mentors. The most recent entry to this series, *A Better Man*, offers this beautiful advice: "Before speaking . . . you might want to ask yourself three questions: Is it true? Is it kind? Does it need to be said?"

The last one has changed my behavior in a way that no one will notice but me. Others won't know that I didn't say what I was thinking because

I realized it didn't need to be said and didn't say it. All those unnecessary comments consigned to the wind.

Gamache also offers four sentences we must learn to say and mean. He holds up a finger for each one.

- I don't know.
- I need help.
- I'm sorry.
- I was wrong.

These are rare and beautiful things to say and wonderful to hear. Especially "I was wrong."

HOW NOT TO APOLOGIZE

Not only do many of us resist apologizing, but when we do, it's a feeble attempt that doesn't even begin to land with the person to whom we are apologizing. Here is what not to do:

- **IF YOU SAID OR DID SOMETHING HURTFUL TO YOUR PARTNER, DO *NOT* SAY, "I'M SORRY YOU FEEL THAT WAY."** That is not an apology and there is zero responsibility here for whatever you did. Whenever someone has said this to me, my response is: "Don't be sorry I feel this way. Be sorry about what you did/said that caused me to feel this way, and please be specific so that I know you understand what happened here." What follows is usually far more honest and impactful.
- **DON'T DEMAND AN APOLOGY.** If you get one under those circumstances, it won't be sincere and may even make things worse. I agree with Robert Brault, a freelance writer whose observations are frequently quoted. He wrote: "Life becomes easier when you learn to accept an apology you never got." This has been true for me. Although I may believe that I am owed an apology, if I spend any energy resenting the fact that it is unlikely to happen, it would

be like a rock in my shoe. Once I accept the apology I believe that person's higher self would make, the wound heals and my peace is restored.

- **DO NOT RUIN AN APOLOGY BY TACKING ON AN EXCUSE.** If your apology is followed by an excuse or an explanation of why you did whatever you did, your partner can expect that you'll likely repeat the thing you just apologized for. If what you did deserves an apology, just apologize. Your reasons don't matter. And don't do it again.

- **DO NOT APOLOGIZE FOR YOUR EMOTIONS.** As in, "I'm sorry I'm crying" or "I'm sorry I'm so upset" or "I'm sorry, but I'm really angry." When you do, you're apologizing for being real. Own those emotions, name them. To quietly say, "I'm angry," is powerful. Just don't act it out.

- **DO NOT BLAME OTHERS FOR SOMETHING THAT HAS YOUR FIN-GERPRINTS ALL OVER IT.** Above all, do not use the passive voice so popular with politicians, as in, "Mistakes were made." Really? Gosh, wouldn't it be nice if those pesky mistakes would stop making themselves! For example, if someone says, "I realize this could have been done better," there is no actor here. A more honest comment would be, "I could and should have done this better."

 ## The Conversation: It's Not You, It's Me

It can be hard to confront our earlier selves, thinking back to all the times when we did or said things that were unkind or thoughtless. Hard to admit that sometimes we cared more about being right than being a loving partner. Take heart. You can make up your mind to be kind and truthful going forward. It truly is a decision you can make. Don't mistake being kind for being weak or soft. Kindness is a strength. It can allow us to navigate a rough passage. It can move mountains.

Here are examples of what you might say if you know an apology is in order:

"I love you. I am so sorry I said that, did that. It was unkind and insensitive. Please forgive me."

Or . . .

"I am so sorry I told the guys I'd golf with them this weekend. I've called and canceled. I know you want to go to Jubilee Farm with the kids and get pumpkins for Halloween, and that's what we are going to do. I was wrong to make other plans. Sometimes I can be selfish. I don't like that about myself and I promise to do better. Nothing is more important than doing things with you and the kids. Forgive me?"

Or even . . .

"I recognize something about myself. I've come to terms with the fact that a long-term commitment just isn't a goal for me, and I apologize for making you think that it was. I know you want a partner for life, and you deserve to have that. I'm sorry I can't be that person. I hope you'll forgive me if I've wasted your time."

I could write a dozen scripts, but you know what apology might have your name on it. If you recognize there is a need to apologize, please do it.

17

Conversation 7: It's Not Me, It's You

We are prepared, including legally, to fire you for a bad attitude.
—HERB KELLEHER, FOUNDER OF SOUTHWEST AIRLINES

When a relationship ended, you may have been assured, "It's not you, it's me." This may have left you baffled, with nowhere to go, because you're pretty sure that it *was* really about you. We would have welcomed or at least endured a loving chastisement, and perhaps we would have made a necessary shift in our behavior, but we weren't given a heads-up.

While dread of giving or receiving feedback is understandable, it is also puzzling, because if I asked you what you would want your partner to do if he or she thought you were the best thing that ever happened to him or her, you would say, "Tell me!" Right? And if I asked what you would want your partner to do if he/she was wounded or angered by something you had said or done, you would say (at least I *think* you would say), "Tell me!" even if it would be hard to hear. If a problem exists, it exists whether we talk about it or not, so we might as well talk about it. After all, we can't fix a problem we don't know about!

> If a problem exists, it exists whether we talk about it or not, so we might as well talk about it.

We could all benefit from occasional feedback. Most of us wouldn't want to settle into old age proudly proclaiming, "Throughout my life, I have not found it necessary to evolve as a human being or to improve myself in any way. I'm awesome!" The trouble is, most people cringe if someone asks, "Would you like some feedback?" Our thought is, *No, I definitely would not like some feedback!* And this is because we think of feedback as criticism, a whole lotta bad news in one sentence.

STAYING AWAKE DURING "GRADUALLY"

The most important thing to consider if you feel uncomfortable giving feedback is that you need to make the success of your relationship more important than comfort. If you and your partner don't talk about things that disturb you, one or both of you may eventually blow up. The goal of feedback is ensuring that you and your partner won't arrive at any negative "suddenlys."

We give feedback when we let our partner know that something they've done or said concerns us. It's pointing out something and asking what's going on. It's letting our partner know that we didn't love what they did or said and we'd prefer they didn't do it again. Confronting requires a more serious conversation. The bar is raised. Something has to change. In this chapter I will walk you through how to give feedback. In the next chapter I'll walk you through how to confront. The chart on the next page may be useful in determining which situations warrant a confrontation and which simply require feedback.

But before we look at how to give feedback, let's begin by looking at ourselves. Since we are not on the receiving end of ourselves, we may be unaware that, although our message might be right on, our delivery leaves something to be desired. Take a moment and recall a time when you were upset with your partner. What did you say? What was your tone of voice? Did you raise your voice? Did you curse? What was the expression on your face?

FEEDBACK	CONFRONTATION
It's never happened before and I don't think my partner was aware that he or she did it.	There is a pattern of similar behavior. I've said something and nothing is changing or not changing quickly enough.
I see a pattern that could become a problem later on and want to share it with my partner so that he or she has an opportunity to course correct.	My partner has done something so upsetting that even once is too much.
Something happened once, I do not necessarily have an expectation that my partner changes, but I want to make sure he or she sees it from my perspective.	Something keeps happening and now it is affecting our relationship.
A mistake was made and it's important to share insights on what could have been done better.	Mistakes keep being made and there is an underlying issue that needs to be explored and corrected to prevent further, unanticipated damage to our relationship.

Now ask yourself what it would have been like to be on the receiving end of you in that moment. Would you have fallen into the traditional mode of fight or flight or would you have invited a conversation so that you could understand why your partner was unhappy, upset? Would you have felt loved, cherished, valued?

My friend, let's call her Michelle, frequently struggles to resolve fights with her husband. She never remembers what he says, just how she feels when he says it. Later, he is angry at her withdrawal. "This is stupid. I didn't say anything worth barricading yourself in here all day!"

Yes, you did, she thinks, *but I can't tell you what it was. I just know that I got the message. What you said. How you said it. Tone of voice. Sarcasm, I think it was. The look on your face. The long-suffering husband. Your back was half-turned to me. Dismissal.*

Michelle feels this in her bones. Angry words crouch behind her teeth, ready and willing. He sees the flash in her eyes and knows to stop, then pretends later that this is silly. *Silly woman, upset for no reason.*

"He says he values my intelligence, but he doesn't reach for me. Doesn't touch me." Michelle's primary love language is touch, so when physical expressions of affection ceased, she was confused and hurt. When she tried to communicate this to her husband, her fear and anger triggered both of them and they added another topic to their list of indiscussables as their mask of civility wore thinner every day.

After one of their fights, Michelle called her husband on his cell phone, hoping for some hint of clarity or resolution. Their connection kept going in and out, and there was a lot of static on the line. Michelle kept shouting, "Are you there? Can you hear me?" Later, she realized it was a perfect metaphor for their inability to communicate about troubling issues.

Their constant sniping at each other reminded me of a passage from the novel *The Miniaturist* by the English actress and author Jessie Burton. "This is not a conversation; it is Agnes sending out darts and watching them pierce."

Michelle's marriage failed. Slowly. Surely. What was needed was a series of conversations, during which each of them took responsibility for their emotional wake and the understanding that none of us is just one thing. When choosing a long-term partner, you are choosing a set of problems you'll be grappling with long-term. Nobody's perfect. We are good and bad, energized and lazy, hilarious and boring, simple and complicated, happy and sad, frightened and courageous. Our challenge is to love the whole person, including the parts that aren't always wonderful. Still, in every relationship issues arise that need to be addressed.

EMOTIONAL WAKE

We've talked about emotional wake, which could be positive or negative, something you remember that warms your heart or something you remember that still hurts. Taking responsibility for our emotional wake doesn't mean we will never ever say anything that might upset our partner. It's just that we will say it in a way that furthers the relationship instead of stopping it in its tracks.

This isn't easy. For most of us, the instant our buttons are pushed, all our hard-won skills fly straight out the window. Our reactions trigger our partners, who do whatever they do when they're triggered, and we quickly arrive at the endgame. We've all been there, done that.

When we are triggered, it is essential to get ourselves untriggered and fight off the tendency to revert to harmful communication tactics, such as name-calling, blaming, or exaggerating.

Each of us is a place where conversations occur. Do you want to be a cozy living room with a crackling fire in the hearth or a basement with dark corners and the smell of damp? Do you want to be described as a mentor, a dementor, a tormentor?

LESSONS FROM A FOUNDRY

Years ago I went to Denver to spend time with Laura Mehmert, a dear friend from high school who is an artist. We went to a foundry where her eight-foot bronze of a cowboy carrying a calf was being poured. In a foundry the crucible holds the molten metal, which is then poured from the crucible into molds to cool and harden so that it can become the work of art conceived by the artist.

I watched as the molten bronze swirled, burbled, hissed, steamed inside the crucible. The question that intrigued me was, "What is that crucible made out of? Why isn't it melting?"

The foundry owner explained, "Most crucibles are made of either clay graphite or silicon carbides—fragile materials, essentially some of the same nonchemical ingredients as in porcelain. If a crucible were dropped on a concrete floor, it would crack or shatter. When a new crucible arrives, I strike it to see if it will ring. If it has a sharp sound, it's okay. If it has a dull, thuddy sound, it's damaged."

He warmed to the topic and continued, "The gold and silver used in computers are refined in crucibles. Your dentist has a crucible. You'll find castings in hospitals, cars, dams, wind generators, cemeteries. Crucibles have a role in forming castings that take people from birth to death."

As do our conversations.

Several weeks after visiting the foundry, I returned to Denver to see Laura's wonderful sculpture, which had been installed in a park near her home in Evergreen, Colorado. We arrived at the park in the early morning. *The Foreman* was magnificent. His long coat blew out behind him, as if he were leaning into a storm. His head was lowered toward the calf safe in his arms. The calf seemed vulnerable, yet its eyes were soft, not frightened. As I walked around *The Foreman*, touching it, marveling at its beauty, I recalled the crusty crucible in which it had begun to take shape.

I formed a new goal.

My goal was to become a crucible—a strong, resilient vessel in which profound change can safely take place. For my partner, my family, and myself.

In creating a work of art, the crucible has an important job—simply to *hold under extreme heat,* no matter what is poured into it. I relate to the fragility of the crucible. If I get dropped—if, for example, I am given unexpected, harsh feedback—I could get hurt. I could crack or break. I am vulnerable. So are you.

Our relationships are works of art that form one conversation at a time. During an important conversation with your partner, your job is to hold fast so that the two of you are able to discuss what needs discussing, no matter how challenging the topic and no matter how fragile and vulnerable either of you may be feeling at the time.

Before I share *how* to give feedback, how to stop a fight in its tracks, there is something we all need to recognize.

A puzzling human trait is that it is easier to believe bad things about people than good things. We can make ourselves believe anything that suits us, even if it suits us only because it proves us right about something that makes us miserable. Let's admit it. Most of us have spent time brooding darkly about something that happened. In the absence of facts, imagination works overtime. We ascribe motives to the perpetrator, silently build up a head of steam, and finally blow up, shocking our partner who had no clue we were upset.

Remember that little man behind the curtain creating all those special effects, running the show? Your context? When you see or hear something that upsets you, that little man immediately goes to work and often sets us up for a dark day and a conversation with our partner that will end up in the dank basement. Elizabeth Berg said this beautifully in *Tapestry of Fortunes*. "Wherever we are in the world, we mostly live in the small space between our ears."

Simply put, we make up stories about people and behave as if our stories are true.

> We make up stories about people and behave as if our stories are true.

We all do this. The question we should ask ourselves is, Does the story I'm telling myself about my partner have any basis in fact? What do I gain when I put a negative interpretation on my partner's words and actions? What do I win by doing this, and is that what I really want?

I have found that asking your partner a question consisting of eight magic words costs less than telling a story. I'll tell you what that question is, but first my friend Jim tells this story.

JIM AND BRENDA

I was preparing for a business trip. I told my wife, Brenda, that I needed for her to handle something for me while I was gone. There was a deadline involved, and it had to be done by a certain date or I would miss out on whatever it was. My schedule would have made it hard for me to take care of it. Brenda said she'd do it, not to worry. I reminded her as I was leaving, and she reassured me she'd get it done.

When I got home, after hugs and chitchat, I asked her about the thing she had promised to handle. Her face froze. "Oh, Jim. I'm so sorry. I forgot all about it."

I stared. "You *forgot?*"

She said, "Yes, I'm so sorry! I was working on an art project and it completely slipped my mind."

"I can't believe this," I said. "I. Can. Not. Believe. This! I told you how important this was, and you promised you'd handle it. If you love me, how could you let that happen!"

143

Tears filled Brenda's eyes. "I love you. I just . . . I know it was important." She moved toward me. I moved away.

"Brenda! If you love someone, you don't forget something that important, something you promised to do."

Brenda took in my face, my tense body, my anger, and quietly asked a brilliant question. "Jim, what will you win if you win this argument?"

Jim stopped and it hit him. If he won that argument, his prize would be the belief that his wife didn't love him. Nothing could have been further from the truth and he knew it. Why would he want to succeed in convincing himself and the light and joy of his life, the center of his heart, that she didn't love him?

Have you told yourself a story about your partner that causes sadness, anger, or pain? What argument are you waging? What are you trying to be right about? If you win your argument, what's the prize?

I thought about this recently as I worked myself into a righteous rage over the way a family member had behaved toward me, reviewing all the reasons why I was justified to feel the way I felt, to believe what I believed, and to take the steps I was considering.

And then I remembered Brenda's question. "What do you win if you win this argument?"

Estrangement. Bitterness.

Please, dear God, let me lose this argument. And all similar arguments in the future.

Jim's story kicks me in the gut every time I think of it. Why do we do things, say things, that will inevitably take us to some dark, hurtful place? What are our reasons for inflicting pain? Doesn't love do its best not to hurt others?

FOUR QUESTIONS TO ASK YOURSELF
BEFORE GIVING FEEDBACK

We've all heard that feedback is a gift, yet most of us have received feedback that felt more like a bad mood looking for a place to land. Or like undeserved criticism—the opposite of a gift. If you are the gift-giver, there are four questions to ask yourself before you proceed:

1. If I were to receive this gift, what might I feel? Is this the right gift, the best gift, or the right timing for this gift?
This is important to ponder to ensure your feedback is well received and not returned to the store or even regifted to *you*.

2. What is my intention?
An objective of feedback is to enrich your relationship. With this in mind, is your feedback valid, honest, and focused on helping your partner? Or are you giving this feedback to show how right you are and how wrong your partner is? Might this feedback feel like a gift or an attack?

3. Am I making assumptions about my partner's comment or behavior that might be incorrect, off base?
What are the facts of the situation as you know them? If you are unsure or can't know for certain until you talk with your partner, then frame your feedback as an observation rather than a fact.

4. Have my partner and I clarified the conditions that are essential for our relationship to thrive?
Have you been consistent in your expectations? Are you giving feedback today about something you responded to differently yesterday or have overlooked in the past? Have you made the mistake of thinking your partner should know what you would have liked for him or her to do?

And what about your attitude?

In an argument, do you exhibit a pervasive sense of self-importance in which you view your assumptions, your personal philosophies, your opinions as correct? When someone dares to challenge you, do you skip defense and go straight to offense, suffocating the opinions of others, in this case your partner?

During disagreements, what puts most of us off is rigid thinking. The conversation quickly deteriorates if one of us is unmovable. What's the point? When the conversation screeches to a halt because one of us gives up and capitulates, there will likely be resentment, and the one who acquiesces without putting forth his or her view will smolder.

There's a much better way to go! The following story illustrates where feedback typically goes wrong and offers a simple but profound alternative that turns what could feel like an attack into a loving conversation.

ALICE AND TODD

Alice and her partner, Todd, were having dinner with friends at a restaurant. As Alice began to share her ideas about an upcoming project at work, Todd leaned back in his chair and yawned. When Alice's friends expressed enthusiasm about her idea, Todd stayed silent. In fact, he seemed disengaged throughout the meal. Alice was hurt, embarrassed.

When they left the restaurant and said goodbye to their friends, Alice turned on Todd. "I can't believe how rude you were tonight! You obviously don't care about me or the project I'm working on."

Todd was stunned to see tears spilling from Alice's eyes. "What, are you crazy? I *do* care. You know I care."

"Yeah, right! That's why you yawned when I started talking about it. You didn't pay any attention, didn't even look at me. It's like you weren't even there."

"Oh baby, I'm sorry! You're right. I couldn't focus tonight. I was going to tell you later. I got laid off today."

End of attack. Alice had misinterpreted Todd's behavior and behaved as if her interpretation, her story, was true. How different it would have been if she had said: "Tonight when I started talking about my work project, you yawned, and for the rest of the evening it was as if you really weren't listening and didn't care about what I was saying. Can you tell me what is going on?"

Alice could even have said something during dinner in front of their friends. "Todd, you seem distracted, uninterested. Can you tell us what is going on?"

If Todd had shared that he had just lost his job, Alice and their friends would have immediately wanted to console and encourage him. No angst, no anger, no story.

The challenge is to catch yourself in the act of making up a story about *why* your partner did or said what he/she did or said, especially if you are convinced the story you are telling yourself is true. Ask yourself, *Could I be wrong?*

Consider that the stories you tell yourself make you happy or they make you angry, resentful, sad, or anxious. What if those stories are bogus?

EIGHT MAGIC WORDS

Doubt is a gift and those who never doubt their beliefs or opinions are not much fun to be around. One thing I've learned about love is that nothing is ever what it seems. Instead of launching into the story you have told yourself, what if you briefly described what you observed or heard and then asked: *"Can you tell me what is going on?"*

These are the eight magic words. This is how to stop wasting all those hours, days, and weeks stewing about something that may or may not be true. This is how to prevent a fight and, instead, have a conversation. This is how to stay current with your partner during the "gradually" part of your lives together.

You are being fierce in that you are *asking before telling*. You are *listening before talking*. For example, perhaps you might say, "This weekend you turned down Gary's invitation to golf and my invitation to go to a movie. Lately you've spent most of your time on the sofa watching TV and complaining about work. Can you tell me what is going on?"

You don't say, "Well, you're no fun. You're turning into a lazy bum." And you haven't avoided the topic. You've laid it on the table, without an interpretation on top of it. You're simply saying, "This is what I saw or heard. Talk to me."

I had a funny example of this happen at work. I overheard one of our sales reps yelling on the phone, and it was clear a customer was on the other end. I was horrified, but using the fierce approach, when he hung up, I said, "I'm pretty sure that was a customer you were yelling at. Can you tell me what was going on?" "Yes," he said. "She's losing her hearing and won't wear hearing aids. She keeps saying, 'Talk louder. Talk louder.' And I always end up yelling. It's exhausting, but I love her. She's great."

RECEIVING FEEDBACK

It's important that feedback goes both ways, so what about the feedback your partner gives you? Receiving feedback gracefully is one of the hardest things to do. When we learn we have behaviors that may need correcting, it often takes us by surprise and can be difficult to hear.

For example, have you ever received a gift that made you wonder what the gift-giver was thinking when they purchased it for you? I'll never forget opening the Christmas present my mother mailed to me when I was a young mother. My family watched as I lifted the lid of the box. My smile turned to confusion. In a quavering voice, one of my daughters asked, "What is it?" I wondered if we'd need to feed it, hang it on the wall, or return it with a note. "Did you mean to send me a box of compost?"

Turns out it was a sweater, hand-knitted by my mother, unique in the world. It resembled a nest of twigs, leaves, and various detritus from the forest floor. It was oversized, camouflaged. I could have camped out in it. The only person I could imagine wearing it was my favorite wizard, Radagast the Brown, from *The Lord of the Rings*. I never wore it in public but came to love it because my mother made it.

Feedback can be like that. I think at times we all receive feedback that doesn't resonate with us right away. *I'm not like that!* Sometimes the feedback can be off the mark. *I am* really *not like that!* Other times we receive a gift that we never would have bought for ourselves, and it turns out to be one of the best gifts we receive. I confess that it often takes me a while to recognize the truth in the feedback I've received.

Even when the delivery is off-putting, the question to ask yourself is, "Have I received feedback like this before? Maybe there is something to this 'gift' that I need to take a second look at."

We will enrich the relationship with our partner by leaning in, getting curious, and asking clarifying questions so that we more fully understand the feedback. This is often surprising for the feedback giver and creates a positive cycle of giving and receiving feedback between both of you.

If the delivery is harsh and involves a raised voice, I suggest saying: "I want to hear what you have to say. I want to understand what has angered you, but I need you to find a different way to talk to me."

If the feedback feels too general, vague, or inaccurate:

- **ASK FOR CLARIFICATION AND EXAMPLES.** "Can you provide the specific details that led to this feedback? When did it happen? Where did it happen?"
- **EXPLORE YOUR PARTNER'S INTERPRETATION.** Don't just assume you understand exactly what your partner means when he or she tells you something. Remember, just like you, your partner has a little man behind the curtain creating all kinds of special effects. Your partner may have got it right or may have totally misinterpreted you. Ask, "How did you interpret what I said, what I did?"
- **LISTEN TO THE SPECIFICS IN THE FEEDBACK.** What is your partner trying to convey? Is this a current situation or has your partner been sitting on the feedback for a while?
- **LET YOUR PARTNER FINISH HIS/HER THOUGHTS.** Don't interrupt. Focus on trying to understand.
- **TAKE RESPONSIBILITY FOR THE IMPACT.** Even if the impact was not your intention, accept your part in it. Apologize if needed and appropriate.
- **IF YOU GET TRIGGERED, ADMIT IT.** You can ask to stop the conversation and come back to it later if you need time to calm down and collect your thoughts.
- **PARAPHRASE WHAT YOU HEARD AND DISCUSSED AND COMMIT TO ACTION IN THE AREA YOU ARE WILLING TO CHANGE.** Clearly articulate what you have learned from the feedback. You don't have to decide anything then—just listen. If you need time to process the feedback, let your partner know and make certain you follow up.
- **SINCERELY THANK YOUR PARTNER FOR GIVING YOU THE FEED-BACK.** Partners who receive feedback with curiosity, grace, and gratitude are well on the path to creating love every day. I'm not

suggesting any of this is easy. There's always a risk. A magnet on my refrigerator door says: "They would have passed a pleasant evening had crap not gotten real." I laugh every time I see it.

The most important thing I want you to understand is that feedback keeps you and your partner current during "gradually."

Remember my friend Jim? He was standing in his front yard with a friend. As he looked over the fence at the luscious roses and weed-free lawn in his neighbor's yard, he said, "Boy, I wish I had her yard."

His friend said, "If you had her yard, in about two weeks it would look like your yard."

Jim stared at his friend, who explained. "She does things to her yard that you don't do to yours. When she sees a weed, she pulls it. When you see a weed, you resent it."

This was true, and as his weeds grew, they invited relatives over and before long, they had taken over.

Remember, feedback includes sharing what you appreciate about something your partner said or did. It's a way to care for your relationship, to tend to it every day.

Okay, let's do it. Here's your homework.

 ## The Conversation: It's Not Me, It's You

The following guidelines may be useful. The steps are *when, where, what, explore,* and, if needed, *why.* The trajectory of feedback goes something like this.

Begin by providing context for this feedback. *When, where,* and *what* did you see? Describe what happened or what your partner did just like a video camera would capture it, without using loaded words. *What* did they do or say that you feel is important to give feedback about? *What* did you observe?

Let's say you went to lunch with your partner. She kept

looking at her cell phone, and just when your meal had been served, she leapt up and hurried outside. She was gone for a long time. When she finally returned, you were not feeling appreciated. If you used the fierce approach, you might say something like this:

> When we agreed to meet for lunch yesterday, I was really looking forward to our time together. But when your phone rang just as our food arrived, you stepped outside to take the call and it lasted for quite a while. By the time you returned, your meal was cold.
>
> You seem distracted, and we don't have much time before we need to get back to work. Can you tell me what is going on?

Your partner may apologize and give you a perfectly reasonable answer: "I'm sorry! I should have told you I might have to take a call from the vet. My cat is really sick and she called to give me a diagnosis and the treatment plan."

But what if she doesn't see the problem? What if she says something like, "Well, as you can imagine, I've got a lot on my plate."

Now it's time to briefly (let me emphasize *briefly*) describe the impact for her, for you, for your relationship. *Why* you brought this up.

You could say, "I got the impression that something else was more important than our time together. And when I asked you about the call, you dismissed it in a tone that felt contemptuous. I felt shut down, shut out. The result, whether you intended it or not, is that I'm not eager to spend time with you right now. I'd say that's a problem." Remember, we teach people how to treat us.

And what if your partner responded, "I've told you about the project I'm heading up, but I don't think you appreciate what I have to do to keep everyone engaged. I'm worried because we're about to miss a deadline."

There's a deeper issue here. She is triggered and it would be understandable if you immediately got triggered yourself. Don't go there. Remember, if this hasn't happened before, you're in feedback mode, so stay with *explore*.

I hate to admit it, but I think you're right. I haven't understood how hard managing this project has been and the level of stress you must be feeling. I'm sorry. Please tell me as much as you can about what you're dealing with.

Can I just say one more time that this isn't easy! To recognize when we are triggered and catch ourselves before we add gasoline to the fire is an act of valor! It takes determination to form a different way of behaving and to practice it so that it becomes habitual, even if you aren't feeling a whole lotta love in the moment.

18

Conversation 8: I Love You, but I Don't Love Our Life Together

The need for change bulldozed a road down the middle of my mind.
—MAYA ANGELOU

Last year I had shoulder surgery. I had lived with a torn rotator cuff for years, and if any of you have lived with chronic pain, you know how exhausting it can be. I delayed surgery, but finally my life was compromised to the point where something had to change. Recovery was long and painful, but today my body is much happier and I have resumed the activities I enjoyed before my shoulder and I had a falling-out.

Chronic pain in a relationship is also exhausting. The relationship loses strength, loses its ability to withstand and bounce back from tough times, gets sicker with each missing or failed conversation. And still we remain, even when we are certain we have arrived at the beginning of the end. So why do so many unhappy people stay together?

Some reasons might be

- financial dependence;
- for the sake of the kids/grandkids;
- spiritual convictions;
- fear of being alone ("No one else would want me.");
- loss of sense of self ("Who would I be without my partner?");
- denial ("It's not so bad."); or
- the devil you know. . . .

If any of these strike a chord with you, I hope you will be honest with yourself about how happy you are or aren't, consider that your partner is probably unhappy as well, and prepare for the conversation the two of you need to have, even if you dread the aftermath.

You may believe that there is no way to reach your partner and are beginning to think of your life as before and after. I would ask you to remember that you loved this person at one time, enough to commit to him or her, so before you decide to leave, let's give it one last shot.

In the previous chapter you learned how to give feedback. If your feedback has fallen on deaf ears and nothing has changed, it's time to notch things up.

In this chapter you will learn how to have a come-to-God talk with your partner about something that must change. Emphasis on *must*. This conversation will let your partner know that the end may be in sight. You're not there yet, but you can see it from here, and you are offering your partner one more opportunity to help you fix what's broken. After all, there can be no alliance if the only way a relationship can continue would require a distorting compromise to the detriment of one or the other.

Because there is so much at stake in this conversation and because it's the one that scares people the most, I will tell you two true stories and outline their invitations to their partners to have these conversations. So if you're teetering on the edge of your relationship, you can prepare for one of your own.

STORY 1: TOM AND MYKEL

Let me introduce you to Tom and Mykel, a couple with whom I was enjoying dinner at a restaurant when a fight broke out. I had noticed that for Tom and Mykel, arguing was their default mode, almost the family business. This was a genuine fight. I've captured the conversation as I recall it.

Tom announced that he had bought a boat and handed Mykel a glossy brochure. Mykel stared at the brochure, handed it to me, then turned to Tom and said:

M: Have you lost your mind! [This wasn't really a question.]

T: Whaddya mean? It's beautiful. She's perfect for taking clients for a cruise.

M: Well, I won't be with you because, in case you've forgotten, I get seasick, so this would be one more reason why we don't spend time together.

T: There are pills you can take. Come on, Mykel. Tell me you don't love this boat. Look at the teak.

Mykel put her head in her hands. Tom looked at me, silently pleading, *Can you help me out here?* I shook my head. Mykel raised her head.

M: What do you want, Tom? This is another thing we don't need and can't afford.

T: No, what do *you* want, Mykel? What about you with your Botox and fake eyelashes? You're always off to the eyelash person so you can look like two tarantulas have camped on your face. I don't like them, Mykel. They're ridiculous. I liked the natural you, but you never asked me what I thought. And what about you in your Calvin Klein jeans, wearing your what—Giorgio Armani—glasses. And how many credit cards do you have, for God's sake!

Right about this time, I made myself as invisible as possible. Mykel seemed stunned. Tom took a big drink of his wine, and Mykel stared at her plate.

M: I've wanted to look good for *you*, Tom. I wanted you to want me. We haven't made love in a long time. That's why the eyelashes and the clothes. I know I spend too much. You're right, but honestly, at this point in my life, I don't want more of anything. I want more of us, you and me.

Tom looked away and Mykel's shoulders slumped. She sat back and sighed.

M: What I don't want is to entertain clients on a boat. I don't even like most of your clients. That guy we had dinner with last week is a monomaniac.
T: Agreed, but one who pays our bills, pays for the lifestyle you enjoy, and be honest, you don't want to spend time with me. You'd rather spend time with your friends.

Mykel sat back, took a deep breath, and then spoke quietly.

M: I do love time with my friends, but I want to spend time with you, Tom, and that is almost impossible because of the demands your clients make on you. We have your clients to thank for the nightmare that is called our life these days. You're on your phone all the time, available to them 24/7. I feel like you're a kept man and not by me. You're here but not here. It may shock you to know that I don't love our lifestyle. I would like to have coffee with you in the morning and take a long walk with the dogs. I want us to spend more time together. We could go away for a weekend, have a romantic dinner now and then.
T: I'm not going back to when I carried a brown bag in my briefcase and people looked at me sideways like I had something stuck in my teeth.
M: Yeah, well, that was the man I fell in love with. That man made me happy.
T: You've sure got an unhappy way of being happy.

Mykel's face flushed.

M: I know. I'm sorry. That's because I'm not happy, and I don't think you're happy either. I don't even know if you care about me or your friends anymore. Last week when we attended the funeral for Rick's father, everybody was walking by the open casket and people were crying and you whispered, "That jerk looks dead!"

Tom laughed.

M: It's not funny! You'll probably die reading a book on how to get rich quick.

T: You wanted dinner. We're having dinner. Why are you so angry? What did I do?

M: In case you didn't know, Tom, being a self-absorbed egomaniac is not an actual job description!

It was like watching a car crash. The fight screeched to a halt when they both turned to me, two beautiful catastrophes, jaws clenched, eyes flashing. They wanted help. I figured we wouldn't be ordering dessert. Dang!

SMALL DIMINISHMENTS, SMALL ANNOYANCES

Can you detect the layers of unaddressed, unresolved issues that led to this fight? You have to wonder if this marriage will survive. No agreement on goals for their lives. Money—who spends what on what. She reads *Architectural Digest*. He reads *Modern Mercenary*. Little time together, but guilt, love, and longing expressed by Mykel, unacknowledged by Tom. Somewhere along the way, Tom and Mykel lost the plot and their once great romance devolved into a division of duties and then into a story about two people just trying to make it from day to day.

The widest gulf in a marriage is the distance between getting by and not quite getting by. Small annoyances accumulate until gradually, gradually,

gradually, one missing conversation at a time, a couple crosses that gulf and arrives at an explosive, ugly "suddenly." It must have been painful as quietly, ignoring the signs, Tom and Mykel's marriage lost direction and found itself searching for meaning. It was easy to see where their success had led them, but I wondered what it had kept from them.

Fredrik Backman describes a conversation between a couple not so unlike Mykel and Tom in *A Man Called Ove*:

> It was more an argument where the little disagreements had ended up so entangled that every new word was treacherously booby-trapped, and in the end it wasn't possible to open one's mouth at all without setting off at least four unexploded mines from earlier conflicts. It was the sort of argument that had just run, and run, and run.

Mykel and Tom could no longer avoid the conversation that had been waiting in the wings. They were faced with the conversation they'd been avoiding, the conversation that would help them find a way forward, that felt right to both of them, or would help them realize they had strikingly different, incompatible goals for the future, and it was time to say goodbye.

The challenge was to name the issue at the heart of their difficulty. (Grendel's mother. Remember her?) If they didn't, they would continue sniping at each other and nothing would change. (Spoiler alert: Tom and Mykel are still together, but more on that later.)

Believe me, I understand the dread. It's easy to confront a tough issue with your partner when he or she isn't in the room. When your partner is sitting opposite you, that's another thing entirely.

Because of past experience, when we envision being confronted, we usually picture someone in our face, finger pointed, saying *you, you, you*. No one's idea of helpful. And when we imagine confronting someone ourselves, we fear we will get emotional (we will), our partner will get triggered (very possibly), and things will head south in a heartbeat (been there, done that). Why would anyone sign up for that?

If your stomach flips at the thought of confronting your partner's behavior, you're in excellent company. It is far less threatening to talk with friends about our frustrations, which doesn't change anything, than to look into your partner's eyes and address the specific behavior that is causing the relationship to decline.

A WELL-DESERVED BAD RAP

The problem most of us face is that all of our attempts to date have failed miserably. We don't know how to make it better this time, and the stakes are high. We sense that a monster is lurking in the bushes, but today is not the day we are prepared to take it on, not the hill on which we're prepared to die. Our fears may include:

- A confrontation could escalate the problem rather than resolve it.
- I could lose the relationship.
- Confronting the behavior could force an outcome for which I am not prepared.
- I could incur retaliation.
- I may not be taken seriously.
- The cure could be worse than the disease.
- I could be met with irrationality or emotional outbursts.
- I could discover that I am part of the problem.

All of these fears are valid and yet the results of not confronting a problem include:

- The problem could escalate rather than be resolved.
- I could lose the relationship.
- I could discover that I am part of the problem.

You get the drift.

The very outcomes we fear if we confront someone's behavior are practically

The very outcomes we fear if we confront someone's behavior are practically guaranteed to show up if we don't.

guaranteed to show up if we don't. It will just take longer, and the results will likely occur at the worst possible moment, when we are least expecting it, with a huge price tag attached.

REPOSITIONING
CONFRONTATION

It's not the message that's the problem; it's the delivery. I want you to have a simple, powerful, clear approach that will be highly effective no matter the issue or the personality you are confronting. One that will allow you to remain grounded, calm, and clear. Not an attack. A conversation. Before I walk you through this conversation, it's important to take the curse off the idea of confrontation.

The word *confront* begins with *con*, which means "with" in Spanish, and ends with *front*. To confront someone is to be *with* that person *in front* of an issue rather than firing at someone from across the room or slipping into a vindictive silence. It's as if you are side by side, holding flashlights, shining a light on an issue together. It isn't an opportunity to say hurtful things. What we say is important. *How* we say it is equally important.

Fierce conversations fade and die because we don't confess even to ourselves—much less to others—that we are not always operating from a base camp of love and harmony. There are occasionally dark instincts at play. Like jealousy, fear, revenge.

Being human is hard! I remember reading C. S. Lewis's *Surprised by Joy*. Looking inside himself, Lewis found "a zoo of lusts, a bedlam of ambitions, a nursery of fears, a harem of fondled hatreds." I felt elated and absolved. Was it possible that the people I admired—the good, wise people of the world—were at times like me?

The emotions to which C. S. Lewis admitted are natural and exquisitely useful feelings to have and to say. It's human to be angry and it's okay to tell someone what you're feeling. Otherwise, if you serve up all your angst and fire boiled down to a pablum, you may induce profound indifference. Saying "I am angry" is powerful *as long as* you are not yelling and pointing a finger at someone's nose.

COMMON BUT FATAL MISTAKES

Think of something your partner does (or doesn't do) that you want to confront, and imagine what you would say to him or her. Then identify your unique fingerprint—the load it would be tempting to attach to the message. Typical loads are . . .

- Blaming (my all-time favorite, the mother of all loads). "This whole thing is your fault." "You really screwed this up."
- Name-calling, labeling. "You're an insensitive narcissist." "You're a liar." "You're a failure."
- Attaching global weight to tip-of-the-iceberg stuff. This small thing happened and it means this *huge* thing! "You don't love me and never did." "This ruins everything. We're finished."
- Threatening, intimidating (always a winner!). "Guess you don't value this marriage." "You'll never see your kids again." "You do this one more time and . . ."
- Exaggerating. "You always do this." "Never once have you . . ." "This is the hundredth time . . ."
- Pointing to your partner's failure to communicate, assuming a position of superiority, and believing your partner is clearly inferior. "You don't get it." "You can't handle it." "You aren't making any sense at all." "I can't get through to you."
- Saying "If I were you . . ." That's a loaded phrase. If I say that, then you'll feel I'm saying you should have done it my way, which is usually what I'm saying. An additional load embedded in the message is "Why can't you be more like me?"
- Gunnysacking, bringing up a lot of old baggage. "This is just like the time when you . . ."
- Assassinating your partner in public. This is sneaky and cowardly, and we usually try to get away with it by pretending it's funny. "Oh yeah, Janie thinks she's pretty hot stuff!" "Apparently George has all the answers."
- Asking, "Why did you do that?" instead of "What were you trying to do?" *Why* usually triggers people. You'll get a less defensive response with the second question.

- Making blatantly negative facial expressions. Rolling your eyes, shaking your head, frowning.
- Layering your interpretation on something your partner has said or done. "What you really mean is . . ." or "What's really going on is . . ."
- Being unresponsive, refusing to speak, leaving the room. Some would say this is the cruelest load you can attach. The message can be received as "You're dead to me" or "I don't care about you or this issue."

Once we've made the mistakes in this list, once we've blamed, threatened, gunnysacked, delivered a message with a load attached, it's out there. It's not coming back. And what's heartbreaking is that we do these things because we are afraid. Where there is anger, there is almost always fear. We fear this conversation won't go well. We fear there's no rescuing the relationship. We fear our partner might, rightly, point out our considerable contributions to the problem.

You could be right.

You may be thinking, "She can't handle it. She isn't ready," but what most people confess is that it's we ourselves who can't handle it, who aren't ready. It is critical to recognize that *someone* has to handle it or nothing will change. That someone is *you*. Fierce conversations cannot be dependent on how others respond. If you know something must change, then know that it is *you* who must change it. Given what's at stake, you do not have a right to remain silent.

Fierce conversations cannot be dependent on how others respond.

Which is worse: not delivering a message at all or delivering a message with a load attached? Both are disastrous. There is an alternative, but first meet a lovely man.

STORY 2: MY WIFE IS MEAN

Years ago, after giving a talk to a large audience, I met with a small group of leaders for a fireside chat. Each described their struggle with someone at work—a direct report, their boss, a colleague—and asked what they should say to that person. The answer, of course, was that they needed to have the confrontation conversation outlined in chapter 4 of *Fierce Conversations*. In fact, after the fourth person described his issue, everyone shouted, "Chapter 4!" and we all laughed.

The last person to speak surprised us all by saying, "I don't like my wife. She's mean. She's mean to me. She's mean to our daughters. She's mean to our neighbors, our friends. She's a mean person. Cruel, actually. I don't think I can spend the rest of my life with her. What should I say to her?"

It took a few seconds for all of us to recover from such a tortured admission.

Finally I replied, "I am so sorry. It hurts my heart to hear this. While I think this may shock you, I suggest you say to your wife exactly what you just said to us." As the color drained from his face, I added, "Unless you think that asking her what's for dinner will deliver the message." My thought was, *She must be a fire-breathing dragon to elicit that much fear.*

I suggested we talk privately, and during that conversation he struck me as a kind man, a physician, dedicated to healing. But his wife had taught him time and again that he and their daughters dare not bring up her behavior because she would make them regret it. He would pay for any criticism of her. He and their daughters did their best to stay out of firing range. One dysfunctional human being had everyone under her thumb.

Remember that we get what we tolerate. If the physician had stopped his wife in her tracks the first time she said something cruel to him or their daughters, and stuck to his guns no matter how she responded, perhaps they would still be together. (Spoiler alert: they're not.)

He might have used the feedback approach: "What you just said was hurtful and undeserved. Can you tell me what is going on?"

Or "You just shot down our daughter's aspirations. Can you tell me what's going on with the two of you?"

And perhaps ended with, "You need to find a kinder way to speak to us."

The point is, you have talked your relationship into existence, into its current state of struggle. Perhaps you can talk it into something better. And if you can't, at least you will have tried.

Let's assume you have given your partner feedback more than once (if you haven't, back up and start there) and that this feedback has been ignored. Nothing has changed. Now what?

What many people dread the most is how to begin this conversation. I've broken down confrontation into three distinct parts: opening statement, interaction, and resolution. You will say what you have to say in sixty seconds, then invite your partner to respond.

I can hear you thinking, *Sixty seconds? That's not enough time to express all the angst that's been building up inside me. Not enough time to tell the long story I've told and retold myself, plus all the gory details. Not nearly enough time to unleash the emotional diatribe I've rehearsed in my mind.*

But, oh, how powerful it is when a clear, compelling but brief invitation has been prepared and delivered with skill and grace.

OPENING STATEMENT

Preparation and rehearsal of your opening statement is essential. Write down your opening statement and practice saying it. *Out loud.* If you just rehearse it in your head, when the curtain goes up you may be appalled at the words that actually come out of your mouth. There are seven components to an opening statement:

1. Name the issue.
2. Select a specific example that illustrates the behavior you want your partner to change.
3. Describe your emotions about this issue.
4. Clarify what is at stake.
5. Identify your contribution to this problem.
6. Indicate your desire to resolve the issue.
7. Invite your partner to respond.

Let's take these components one at a time.

1. Name the issue.

The problem named is the problem solved. Get right to the point. If you have multiple issues with your partner, ask yourself what's at the core, what's the common theme of all or most of your concerns and frustrations. Do the thinking to identify and name the central issue; otherwise the conversation will lack essential focus and you'll both end up lost and frustrated.

Your invitation should begin with these words: "I want to talk with you about the effect X is having on Y." Notice "I *want* to talk *with* you . . ." versus "I *need* to talk *to* you . . ."

There is a huge difference between "want . . . with" and "need . . . to." Our defenses go up when someone says, "I need to talk to you." If someone needs to talk *to* us, we assume we're expected to shut up and listen. When you say that you want to talk *with* someone, you've indicated the emotional tone with which you're approaching this conversation.

You'll fill in the X and Y.

For example: I want to talk with you about the effect that . . .

- your negativity
- your coldness toward me
- your spending habits
- your refusal to seek help for depression
- your disinterest in physical intimacy
- your drinking

. . . is having on our relationship.

2. Select a specific example that illustrates the behavior you want your partner to change.

Since you've got only sixty seconds for your entire opening statement, this example must be succinct. No long stories. Must you have an example? Absolutely. When someone is upset or disappointed with us but can't think of a specific example that illustrates what is irritating him, his case loses credibility and is easy to dismiss. Take the time to think of an example that hits the nail on the head.

3. Describe your emotions about this issue.

Disclosing your emotions is intimate and disarming. You are letting the person know that you are affected. Contrary to popular opinion, I believe that if you feel angry, you make quite an impact by quietly saying, "I am angry." Perhaps you are concerned, worried, sad, frightened, or frustrated. Name the emotions that are true for you.

4. Clarify what is at stake.

In other words, why is this important? What's likely to occur if nothing changes? What is at stake for your partner, for your family, for the relationship? Use the words *at stake*. Those words have an emotional impact. Say this calmly, quietly. What you say during a confrontation should never be delivered in a threatening manner but communicated simply as a clarification of why it is important.

5. Identify your contribution to this problem.

Before we confront another's behavior, it is essential that we first look at the ends of our own noses. No long confession. What is important is an acknowledgment that you recognize any role you may have played in creating the problem and that you intend to do something about it.

6. Indicate your desire to resolve the issue.

Use the word *resolve*. To say, "I want to resolve this" communicates good intent on your part. There are no divorce papers in a drawer. This is not an ending. In fact, when this approach is used to confront a behavior or issue, more relationships are saved than ended. Additionally, you should restate the issue. That way you will have come full circle, beginning and ending with absolute clarity about the topic on the table.

7. Invite your partner to respond.

When our behavior has been confronted, it may feel as if a court found us guilty and we've simply been called in to learn the date and manner of our execution. In this approach, however, there has been no attack. Instead, there has been a clear statement describing the behavior or issue from your perspective, and you have reassured your partner that you want to resolve the issue. Now you are inviting your partner to join the conversation. For example, "I want to understand what is happening from your perspective. What are your thoughts? What are you feeling?"

By the way, the question I get most often is, "What if the person I need to confront refuses to have the conversation?"

You could say, "What you're not willing to talk about is killing us, so let's talk about it before our relationship dies."

The Conversation: I Love You, but I Don't Love Our Life Together

In Tom and Mykel's case, where do you think we should start? There were many issues that raised their angry heads over dinner. Tom and Mykel could talk about money. They could talk about the relationship and the amount of time they spend together. They could talk about eyelashes. Or don't. It seemed neither of them felt truly loved, cherished, or valued by the other. Tom had issues about his identity and self-worth, having come from tough beginnings and fought his way to where he is now.

Quite often when people spend more money than they have or should spend, they are trying to gift themselves with something that is lacking, and of course material things don't accomplish that. There may be a short-term high, but it quickly fades.

It seemed to me that the core issue for Tom and Mykel was lack of clarification and agreement about goals, not only for their relationship but for their lives going forward. Both were complicit in creating the pain in their marriage.

The next day I helped Mykel prepare for the badly needed conversation with her husband. We timed her invitation to ensure that she could say it in sixty seconds. After much editing, here is Mykel's invitation.

Tom, I want to talk with you about the effect our lack of clarity and agreement on goals for our relationship is having on our marriage.

For example, the cost of this boat will strain our finances, and since I get seasick no matter what I take, this would keep us apart from each other.

I am sad and frightened because there is so much at stake here. If nothing changes, we will be operating on competing agendas for our future, our financial health will suffer, and our marriage may not survive.

I owe you an apology. I love and respect you, but I haven't let you know that often enough. For this I am sorry. I promise to do better.

I want to resolve the effect that our lack of clarity regarding our goals is having on our marriage. Please tell me what you are thinking and feeling.

Let's return to our doctor friend and look at the sixty-second invitation to his wife.

I want to talk with you about the effect your cruel comments are having on our relationship.

When Sherry told us she wanted to study screenwriting, you said that she isn't a good writer and would never get anywhere. When I told you I was thinking about working with Doctors Without Borders, you said that I couldn't even take care of my own family, much less people in a far-off country.

When you say things like this, your daughters and I feel devalued and diminished, which concerns me deeply because there is a great deal at stake. If nothing changes, your daughters may not include you in their lives, may not want to expose their children to your cruel comments. If nothing changes, I can't think of a reason to stay in this marriage, and you may very well end up alone.

I should have let you know each and every time you said something hurtful that it wasn't okay. I apologize for keeping silent.

I want to resolve the effect your cruel comments are having on our relationship. Please talk with me.

Interaction

Once you've extended your invitation, go into listening mode. It is here that the bulk of the conversation takes place. If your partner says something with which you violently disagree, resist the temptation to build a stronger case. Simply listen and ask questions. Say, "I want to understand your thinking, so please say more about that."

We are often severely tested during the interaction phase. Once you've asked your partner to tell you what he or she is thinking, you will ruin everything if you pile on with more examples of wrongdoing on your partner's part. You've said your piece, now get curious. In Mykel's case, it would be important for Tom to recognize what was at stake and to describe his goals for their relationship and for their future. If Tom didn't acknowledge the issue, well, that would make things harder, but at least the issue had been named and it was made clear that, from Mykel's point of view, it was serious.

Sometimes a person has to sleep on it before they really get it. So don't despair if your partner doesn't immediately jump up and say, "You're right, you're right, you're right. Thank you so much for bringing this to my attention."

In fact, since your partner is human like you, he or she may deny, deflect, or defend. For example, in Mykel's case, Tom might have responded in the following ways:

DENY: "I don't know what you're talking about. I wouldn't have done this if we couldn't afford it, and I forgot that you get seasick."

DEFEND: "I am just trying my darndest to give you the life I thought you've always wanted, to do what it takes so that we can hold our heads up high, send our kids to good schools, take vacations. I can't believe you're making me the bad guy here."

DEFLECT: "Well, what about you? I don't get the feeling you want to spend time with me. You're always out and about with your friends, and you spend money like there's no tomorrow."

These responses don't make your partner a bad person, but they can derail the conversation, so your job is to try to keep your partner focused on the effect X is having on Y. If your partner uses any of these techniques, you could say, "We could spend lots of time talking about all of our reasons and excuses for what's going on in our marriage, but what will help us most will be to stay focused on the effect X is having on Y. What are your thoughts about that?"

Being confronted, even with the best intentions and all the right words, can still be so terrifying to some people that they blow up or clam up. If that happens, tell your partner that although you're willing to stop the conversation for now, you will come back to it soon because, as you said, the stakes are high.

What you might say is, "I know you're upset, angry. I'm upset too, but mostly I am concerned because there is so much at stake around this issue. I want to resolve it, and that won't happen by ignoring it. I'm willing to stop the conversation for now and come back to it after you've had time to give it some thought. How about tomorrow evening?"

Resolution

When your partner feels that you fully understand and acknowledge his or her view of reality, move toward resolution, which includes an agreement about what is to happen next. After all, you said your intent was to resolve the issue, and so the following questions will help you accomplish this:

What have we learned?
Where are we now?

Has anything been left unsaid by either of us that needs
saying?
What is needed for resolution?
How can we move forward from here?

End the conversation by making an agreement about the next
steps, about behavior changes needed for both of you, and determine how you will help each other keep your agreements.

Mykel and Tom were both in tears during their conversation.
They were reminded that they loved each other, agreed to put their
marriage first, and committed to changes for both of them.

Sadly, but not surprisingly, the doctor's wife hurled even more
vitriol at him during the conversation and escalated the cruelty
of her comments in the following days, weeks, and months. He
called a year after I met him and told me that he had left the marriage and that he was deeply happy.

Before you prepare for a confrontation, I want to mention Nina
Simone, an African American icon and true diva whose distinctive
voice mesmerized people across five decades. She was a musical
storyteller, and the lyrics in her song "You've Got to Learn" are
profound: "You've got to learn to leave the table when love's no
longer being served."

If a confrontation has your name on it, if love is no longer being
served, write a draft of your sixty-second invitation to the conversation or look up my guide to writing this invitation in *Fierce Love:
A Journal for Couples*.

Say it out loud, see how it feels. Does it ring true? Does it evoke
emotion in you? Time it, edit it, so you don't go over sixty seconds
and you have made it as clear and compelling as possible.

Now "screw your courage to the sticking place," as
Shakespeare put it, and have the conversation.

19

Love After Love

If you can't find one sort of love, Ulf thought, then perhaps there are others out there, to hand, ready to do for you what love has always done for people.

—ALEXANDER MCCALL SMITH, *THE DEPARTMENT OF SENSITIVE CRIMES*

When we commit to someone, we hope our love will endure even as we encounter obstacles—especially when we encounter obstacles. That's my hope for you and the reason I wrote this book. How wonderful it is to spend time with couples who have loved each other through all of their disagreements and grievances. Their bond is unbreakable, and their serenity is beautiful. But sometimes that original, blazing campfire of love has extinguished and we are left with ashes that cannot be rekindled.

If this has happened for you, I hope you can take comfort in the fact that it wasn't for lack of trying on your part. You understand that the conversation is the relationship. Consequently, you let your partner know what you appreciated about him or her. You expressed gratitude, gave and received feedback, apologized when you were in the wrong. You listened deeply when your partner was wrestling with a problem. You clarified conditions, stayed current with your partner, did your best to connect on a deep level, and ensured your own life was working well.

As the marriage continued to struggle, you tried to reach your partner by confronting the issue at the heart of the problems. You've done all you can; nothing has changed. You and your partner fall into the same failings over and over again while doing the backstroke toward Niagara Falls. Over dinner there is a frozen moment in which both of you see what's on the end of your forks.

I want to talk with you about that moment when you know it's truly over, how to exit with love and grace, and what could be available to you on the other side of goodbye.

WHEN THE CONVERSATION STOPS

You know that saying about the straw that broke the camel's back? It's not always something glaring and dramatic that ends a relationship. It may seem small or unreasonable to an outside observer, and yet the incident or comment that triggered the decision to leave a relationship, the "suddenly," occurred after a long string of "graduallys."

For Louise the straw was when she and her husband were walking in the Lake District of England and he said that he'd rather be playing golf. For a friend of mine it was when he discovered that his wife was continuing to buy (and hide) designer clothing even though they were struggling to pay the mortgage and had talked about this many times. For our doctor friend, it was one more hurtful comment directed at their daughter.

For Karen the "suddenly," strangely enough, was a haircut. She had decided to end her relationship with Mark, a man she had been dating, after a vacation with him on Maui. As I listened to Karen, I wished we had discussed the ideas and conversations in this book, but we were casual acquaintances, and the topic hadn't come up. Here is her story, as I recall it.

KAREN AND MARK

He shouldn't have cut his hair. His head was too big for a buzz cut, it wouldn't look good, and he knew I liked his hair a bit long in back. Blond hair over his collar, against his neck. I asked him not to cut it. But he did cut it just before we went to Maui. Came over one day and he looked like he'd been to boot camp. It looked awful, made his head look fat.

And then there were the trade winds. Trade winds are trouble. Nothing to do. Too windy to sit outside. A book's pages practically flying out of my hands. Towels flapping around. Hats wanting to sail away. And once we'd seen all the souvenir shops on Front Street in Lahaina, there was no reason to return.

So there we were. No office to run to, no meetings, errands, mail, email. It gets real quiet in a Kihei condo. Except for the winds blowing, there's nothing to distract except a walk along the beach.

"You mad at me?" he asked after forty minutes of walking with heavy hands.

No, not mad, just far away from you. Feels like I'm leaving you, in my mind. The rest will catch up later.

That's not what I said. I'm a coward. I said, "No."

"Something I've done?"

"I'm not mad."

"Feels like it."

"I'm just . . ." There was quiet. "I don't have anything to say."

We walked the rest of the way in silence, he in front of me, giving me an opportunity to regard the back of his head, his neck, bare of all that gorgeous hair. And while you might think that a haircut is a silly thing to be mad about, during the two years we'd been dating he often did things he knew would upset me, on purpose it seemed. One thing after another. He invited people to join us on dates without asking me. People he knew I didn't like. When I invited him to a celebratory function at my company, he showed up in jeans and a wrinkled shirt even though I had told him it was a formal occasion. He trimmed my labradoodle with kitchen scissors while I was out. When I got home, my poor dog looked like she had mange. He said he wanted to save me the monthly grooming fee I paid to my groomer. I had never complained about that expense, and he knew how much I loved my dog. His own haircut was the one more thing that pushed me over the edge.

I didn't know what to do. I didn't want to tell him we were done. Not on that gorgeous stretch of beach, so the rest of the vacation was painful. I am ashamed to admit that I broke up with him via email a few days after that trip.

When should I have told him what I was feeling? *We don't have anything more to accomplish together. And we aren't really together. We live separate lives. I've never felt so alone as I do in this relationship. Let's acknowledge that we're both unhappy and move on.* But here? Now? On this gorgeous stretch of beach?

IS LEAVING A FAILURE?

Joseph Campbell said that staying in a relationship and giving oneself over to another offers the greatest opportunity for personal evolution, growth. There is wisdom here, truth. But for some there comes a day when the pain is too great, when we've tried and there just isn't anything more to say, when we look at the future and the person we are with isn't in it.

Such a sad moment. And shocking. That moment always sneaks up on us and breaks our heart. *Oh no*, we think. But we can't deny it. When it arrives, it moves in, unpacks, settles in, hunkers down, stares at us from the corners.

In my view, leaving a relationship *is* a failure if we have withheld what we were really thinking and feeling along the way. The conversation *is* the relationship, and this includes feedback whenever we hit a bump in the road. I wish that the first time Mark had done something he knew would upset Karen, she had used the feedback approach. "You invited Jan and Barry to come over without asking me. You know I don't enjoy them. Barry is crude and Jan never stops talking. Can you tell me what is going on?" And if he kept deliberately doing things that upset her, she'd escalate to a confrontation, clarifying for Mark what was likely to happen if he continued behaving that way.

She did make a few feeble attempts to talk about things, but each time Karen felt a door to that conversation was shut in her face, and instead of trying to force it open, she turned and walked away. And soon that day turned to night. And then another day and another. And they moved further apart each day, as she scooted around the edges of her frustration. It was always there, her frustration. At times it would emerge into her consciousness demanding attention, yet each day she said nothing. And nothing. And nothing. Until this silly thing, this haircut, this "suddenly."

Meanwhile, no one can deny that attraction is powerful. Decisions are made in nanoseconds, and we spend years trying to square things up with those decisions, yet when we commit to someone, we have no idea how they or we will turn out down the road.

It seems that marriage is not a destination. If you arrive at marriage, the journey has just begun and you'll have many paths to choose from along the way. Although some people settle into unhappiness, seem to feel at home in it, you may recognize that you have a right to be happy and that although you've done your best, neither you nor your partner is likely to change in ways that would give you both joy.

In her 2016 crime novel *A Banquet of Consequences*, Elizabeth George wrote, "One might argue that if one considers the end of a marriage some sort of personal failure instead of the outcome of arriving at a mutual decision based upon an understanding of differences and an agreement about the future. My first husband and I awakened one morning and realized that aside from an Oxford education, we had nothing in common but a predilection for pizza."

Leaving a relationship is not a failure if you have given it your absolute all, if you've done your best to love and be loved over a long time. Sometimes it is the best decision, the best move you can make. You want a different life for yourself, a different future, and it would be extraordinarily challenging to achieve that if you stay in this relationship. This is also likely true for your partner, who perhaps doesn't have the courage to face this yet.

How can we leave without damaging the one we love, had loved, no longer love?

Perhaps a letter of resignation?

> Dear [blank]: After much deliberation,
> without qualm, scruple, or further delay,
> I hereby tender my formal resignation
> as your lover and future fiancé.
> The job provides too little satisfaction:

too many hours of unneeded duress,
a paucity of productive interaction,
uncertain working conditions, and endless stress.
Pay-wise, I'm undervalued and disenchanted:
advancement's slow, the bonus is routine,
my "on-call" overtime is taken for granted,
and benefits are few and far between.
This document, I'm hopeful, underscores
my deep regret. I'm very truly yours . . . .

—WILLIAM BAER, "LETTER OF RESIGNATION"

Tempting, I know! But that would be cowardly.

I don't take divorce lightly. It's just that sometimes, in spite of our spiritual beliefs, our goals and our efforts, we recognize that parting ways is the best path forward. How do we do that without inflicting more pain when the time comes? Wouldn't it be great if you didn't have to worry about how someone would take it? Wouldn't it be great if you could know they'd be fine, really fine after you left? That they wouldn't crash and burn or turn to alcohol or make your life miserable with arguments about money, co-parenting, or blaming you over and over for everything that went wrong?

If you didn't have to worry about that scenario, you could just say, "It's been so wonderful. You were exactly who and what I needed these past [number] years, and I'd like to think I contributed to your life too. But I think it's clear to both of us that we want entirely different futures, we hold competing values, and we are both miserable. And now we need to go in different directions and work on different things. I will always love you and I am grateful to you." Then make a graceful, loving exit.

Actually, this is exactly what you could say. If you've had the conversations in this book, if you've worked to stay current, if you've paid attention during "gradually," if you've given feedback and asked for it in return, if you've told your partner what you love about him or her—*often*—and if, when nothing changed, you let your partner know what was at stake, then saying it's time to part will not come as a surprise. It may even come as a relief.

Just don't leave in a blaze of angry words and name-calling. Don't take revenge. When a friend learned of her husband's affair, she cut the threads of upholstery in his sports car, sprayed his sports equipment with her perfume, and cleaned the toilet with his toothbrush. I practically gagged when I heard this. On the other hand, don't fold your tent in the night and sneak away like my neighbor. Remember him?

NOW WHAT?

Every time a form requires me to check a box: Single, Married, Divorced, or Mr., Mrs., Ms., I want to check a box that says, "None of your business" or "Irrelevant." In fact, I think there should be no boxes at all. I mean, really, in most cases why should this matter?

What I want to say to you is that love is available in many forms, from all points on the compass, in every moment. It's easy to want another person to fill us up and make us happy, but that's not their job. Forget trying to dream up your ideal mate. Hollywood has already done that for you. Happiness is an inside job. A partner is not required for you to give and receive love. You can always get someone to love you even if you have to do it yourself.

When a relationship fails there's often grieving, but it's grieving for the person you thought someone was. You miss the person you thought they were, but they weren't that person. You're missing someone who never existed. Or you're grieving for the person you thought you would be with your partner. Turns out, you're still the "you" you were before the relationship. No bad guy here.

It's the "now what?" and the fear of being alone that frightens many when they consider leaving a relationship, so I hope to lessen that fear.

I would like you to take the following thought for a walk: there is more than one right way to structure a relationship.

Katharine Hepburn famously said, "Sometimes I wonder if men and women really suit each other. Perhaps they should live next door and just visit now and then."

An important question is, What will give you joy? Perhaps you need to go on a search for joy, fun, laughter, foolishness, a robust sense of humor. If you are unhappy, you leak unhappiness everywhere you go.

I have a lifelong friend who is very successful to all appearances: lots of money, smart kids, loyal wife, and a dog that doesn't bite him. He emails me about all the great stuff happening in his life, about how successful his business is. His kids are in prestigious colleges. His waterfront home has been featured in magazines, and he has caretakers for the grounds. You get the picture. It's as if things just couldn't be better. At the end of a long and very positive-sounding email he wrote, "I'm coming up a little short in the *joy* department, but I can't complain."

> There is more than one right way to structure a relationship.

My friend is a wonderful, kind, smart person who may never know joy. He is very busy living many other people's lives for them. He is not busy living his own life. He has many things and many people to take care of, none of which and none of whom is himself. Although he often invites his wife to go with him on business trips, she typically declines because she has her own set of priorities and finds it difficult to manufacture enthusiasm as he describes his latest clever business coup over dinner. His children find excuses not to spend spring break at home.

I'm sure if you asked him he would say, "My life is very full." A full life is good, it just depends on what it's full of. My friend's life is full of stuff, like the classic hoarder who collects newspapers and has filled most of the rooms in their house with them and can barely squeeze through the stacks. In my friend's case it's not just any newspaper; it's the *Economist* and magazines like the *New Yorker*, *Wine Enthusiast*, *Travel & Leisure*—a much higher quality, but still stuff blocking his way.

I know he wants people to say that they're impressed with all that he has accomplished, but the truth is nobody really looks at his accomplishments but for a passing glimpse, and nobody cares. In fact, during one of our conversations, after he had gone on and on about his belongings—his vacation home in Majorca, his cars, his boat—I finally said, "All these things are totally irrelevant to me. I get no sense of worth or fulfillment from surveying your possessions, and I wish you would stop waving them in my face. I'm kinda busy putting my own life together, and if I am successful, it will not look anything like yours." My comments didn't offend him, nor did they land because he felt I was simply lacking in ambition.

I feel sorry for him, for really, he's alone with his stuff. He has piled it high, climbed to the top, stuck a flag on the summit, and sat down proudly, where he may die of loneliness.

I had lunch with another friend I had not seen for many years. Ever since we were little girls, her goal in life was to be rich. She had been so obsessed with the idea, we had laughed about it. Now, after a long conversation over lunch, I wanted to be supportive of her achievements, so I said, "Well, how does it feel? It seems like you got what you wanted out of life. You have loads of money. You are most definitely rich." She started to cry.

I'm not suggesting that wealth leads to misery. But for us to feel joy, there has to be something more. If we love and are loved, we have the "something more" that makes all the difference.

WHERE MIGHT JOY BE FOUND?

I'm sitting in my car outside the vet's office—because of COVID-19 we aren't allowed to go inside—waiting for them to bring Dobby to me. Dobby is my house elf, a small, red labradoodle with a rash on his back. Meanwhile I'm watching a man standing outside with his dog that is thin, with long legs and short reddish hair, probably a puppy. The dog is so happy its tail almost falls off from wagging. You can tell that he is absolutely joyful in the moment and thrilled to be alive. His tail just wags and wags and wags, and he jumps up and tries to greet every single person who walks past him. It is January but this dog doesn't seem to mind the cold.

I'd like to be that dog for a day. I feel joyful just watching him. If I ever become senile, you may find me walking a dog I no longer have.

Why would I tell you about this dog? Because there is more than one kind of love, and down through the centuries the unconditional, joyful love of a dog has been an enormous comfort to people all over the world. Research shows that people who have dogs live longer, are happier and healthier. (No offense to cat lovers.) I have two dogs: Dobby and Gilly, a Yorkie.

As I sit here writing to you on a Sunday morning, flanked by Dobby and Gilly, I recognize that having a dog doesn't offer comfort if you're struggling with being alone and the possibility that this will not change. What if you always imagined yourself in a relationship, feel you are meant to be in a relationship, but you aren't and there are no candidates on the horizon? What if you've been able to solve everything except the unsolvable, which is that the person you love doesn't or didn't love you in return, or that you couldn't continue to love the person you married no matter how hard you tried?

That was me for several years after my divorce. It took a while before I truly let go of marriage as a goal. I love my daughters, their partners, and my grandchildren, but one day I realized how happy I am, free from romantic attachment and the accompanying requirements.

You will often find me in my tree house on the very top of a small mountain on an island. An essential part of my nature is that I crave heaping handfuls of solitude, and so I changed my life to accommodate a ninety-minute drive from Seattle to Anacortes and a one-hour ferry ride, adjusting my schedule so that I only return to "America," as the islanders say, two weeks each month.

Perched in six Douglas firs, the tree house buoys my spirits. On sunny mornings, I like to stand outside on the deck in my pajamas with a cup of coffee and a pair of field binoculars and observe the waterways below or watch eagles launching from their nests. In the spring I scan the birdhouses I have placed here and there to see if any babies are fledging.

The airy house and its impractical location remind me daily that no one has any claims on me and that, with my temperament, I am not suited to a shared life. I don't care to be constantly, even if benevolently, observed, making it impossible to do anything odd or impulsive—naked gardening, for instance, or getting up at 2:00 a.m. to make myself a cup of cocoa and attempt to write a haiku or two—without provoking the anxious inquiry, "Are you okay?"

I can spend a day reading, catching up on my favorite TV series. I eat what I want when I want. I write, paint, garden, take long walks.

Each day unfolds as I wish it to. It's good.

So, if you can't bear to be alone, please rethink this. There is a difference between being alone and living alone, between living alone and being lonely. In fact, there is nothing lonelier than living with the wrong person.

I'm certainly not against marriage, and I'm not advocating for living alone, but there are millions of people who are deeply happy living by themselves. When you live alone there is peace and quiet, the sound of silence, of your own breathing. Whether you are an introvert or an extrovert, you have friends and family to turn to. You can be as social as you like. In fact, you can be even more social than you were with a partner who didn't particularly like your friends and family or who preferred to stay home while you were dying to get out and do something fun. Get those season tickets to the theater, volunteer to be a docent in an art gallery, visit Loch Ness and see if you can spot Nessie.

Go out and mingle with others, then return to your own space, designed and arranged exactly as you like. Devote time and energy to being a better friend, a better parent or grandparent. Take a class in something that has always called to you. Volunteer in civic organizations, spend time helping an aging neighbor. Take advantage of the freedom, flexibility, and opportunity to focus on your self-realization when you have the time and space to prioritize and please yourself.

As strange as it may sound, living alone can be exhilarating. I suspect that, for many of us, maintaining a home separate from that of our partners, as Hepburn suggested, might strengthen and enrich our relationships.

LOVE AFTER LOVE

Living alone doesn't mean that you won't dip your toe in the dating pool until and unless you become truly happy without a partner. For a few years after my divorce, I would sign up on a dating site for about one week and then cancel my subscription. Welcome to a memorable round of Starbucks meetups.

- First was Tony, an Englishman. "I have a question for you," he said. "In what country are apples indigenous?" "The US, I guess." "Kazakhstan," he explained. "That's interesting," I said. And then he said that there are many different kinds of apples and "Did you know that if you have an apple that you like and plant a seed from it, you wouldn't necessarily get that kind of apple from the seed? You'd have to graft it." "I didn't know that," I said.

- When I thought perhaps we could move to a different topic, he asked, "In what country are potatoes indigenous?" "Ireland?" I ventured. "Everyone says that," he said. "The answer is Peru. They have many different kinds of potatoes. There are orange ones and blue ones and black ones and red ones and white ones and rough ones and smooth ones. There are white ones with black on the inside. There are . . ." *No no no no no*, I screamed inside. The Bubba Gump Shrimp scene from *Forrest Gump* came to mind.

- Next I met Lee. He talked nonstop. Once in a while he would ask me a question about what I did, and when I would start to answer, he would interrupt me and tell me more about himself. Then he would tell me what he thought I did, and I would say, "No, that's not right." And he would say, "Well, I thought that's what you said you do." I would start telling him again, and he would interrupt me and repeat the whole thing over again. Finally I told him I was frustrated that he wasn't allowing me to finish a sentence, much less a paragraph, to explain what it was that I did. He said, "Oh, my daughter tells me that I do that all the time." I figured that at this stage of the game he is not going to change.

- Last was Gus, who pretty much did the same thing—jumped from one story about himself to another in a very meandering way. There was no logic to it. He went into great detail and down many strange paths. He told me a story about almost drowning at Cape Cod because his brain energy was too low, and then he told me about some terrible nightmares he had had a few nights earlier. They were so frightening—skeletons and corpses and a serial killer in his room—that he ended up getting a knife and putting it under his pillow, and now he sleeps with a knife under his pillow every night. Along the way he also told me that he meditates, is a member of the Theosophical Society, and does not watch television. I said I had to go, endured a hug that was too close and too long, and made a beeline out of there.

None of these men talked with me. They talked at me. There was no conversation, just a monologue with little opportunity to respond.

I came home, deleted my profile from the website, and took my dogs for a nice long walk.

You may yet meet a truly wonderful person. I just want you to consider that perhaps, apart from friends and relatives, the person you are most meant to love, to connect with at a deep level, is yourself. Remember that conversation you had with yourself: Is my life working for me? Am I the person I was meant to be? I hope you answered those questions and worked on any parts of your life that haven't been working for you. If there is still work to do, there is no excuse not to do that work now that you have only yourself to consider.

There is something freeing in knowing that your only job is to lead as full, eventful, and joyful a life as you can, so that it doesn't ever feel like you're just waiting around for some magical person to show up in your life. *You* are the magic.

Conclusion

Putting Fierce Love to Work

At the end of a recent interview, I was asked what was at the heart of all things fierce, and I said, "Love." This was an interview about the role of conversations within a corporation, so I explained that we can love our customers, we can love our coworkers, we can love our teammates, our boss, our direct reports, and those with whom we collaborate through-out the organization. Love is not an inappropriate emotion in the workplace; in fact, it makes all the difference. We must love our work, whatever it is. We must love ourselves.

And so, although we have focused on the conversations essential to the success of romantic relationships, the suggestions in this book apply to all of our relationships. Our most valuable currency is not money. Nor is it good looks, charisma, fluency in three-letter acronyms, or multiple degrees. Relationships are our most valuable currency, our emotional capital, which we acquire or squander one conversation at a time.

In my first book, *Fierce Conversations*, I wrote:

> Human connectivity occurs or fails to occur one conversation at a time. In every conversation, meeting, or e-mail we are accumulating or losing emotional capital, building relationships we enjoy or endure with colleagues, bosses, customers, and vendors. In fact, life is about making connections, most importantly, a deep connection with people; otherwise, we do not know what it means to be human.

In case the concept of human connectivity is still unclear, I have asked hundreds of people how they would define human connectivity. I heard:

- practicing empathy
- being understanding
- being transparent
- asking fact-finding questions, showing curiosity
- paying attention to the whole being
- having compassion once you know the story
- being yourself, authentic, genuine
- going deeper with yourself, vulnerability
- having an open mind
- not pushing your own personal agenda
- being clear and direct, no sugarcoating
- responding appropriately
- breaking down us versus them
- acknowledging human imperfection and human experience

Do you see a common theme in that list? Do you relate to the desire for true connection? We are all looking for an invitation to remove our armor and come out from behind ourselves for conversations that allow us to connect with another human being on a deep level. And once that happens, the armor that we carry begins to fall away, piece by piece, and we can see each other as simply human. When we are vulnerable and without defense, there is an opportunity to understand and to be understood, to connect, and to engage in the kind of conversations some of us have managed to avoid having our entire adult lives.

FIERCELY YOURSELF

Our relationships bloom or wilt depending on the love we exchange: its nature, frequency, quality, how freely it's given and received. It can be spoken or unspoken. Gestures, glances, and thoughtful acts are all part of the ongoing conversation between you and your partner. The happiest among us are those who give love at every opportunity, for whom love is the default response, for whom love is something we practice every day.

You may realize that you've learned how to give and receive love or that you've learned how to block it, withhold it. You've learned to respond to unkind words or deeds with anger or you've learned to ask yourself, "What would love do? What would love say? What would love ask?"

Be here, prepared to be nowhere else. You will never have the experience of the Maasai—*I see you. I am here*—if you are glancing at your cell phone, keeping an eye on the television, planning the rest of your day.

Begin listening to yourself as you've never listened before. Begin to overhear yourself avoiding the topic, changing the subject, holding back, telling little lies (and big ones), being imprecise in your language, being uninteresting even to yourself. And at least once *a day*, when something inside you says, "This is an opportunity to be fierce," stop for a moment, take a deep breath, then come out from behind yourself into the conversation and make it real. Say something that is true for you. My friend Ed Brown sometimes stops in midsentence and says, "What I just said isn't quite right. Let me see if I can get closer to what I really want to say." I listen intently to the next words he speaks.

Remember that a careful conversation is a failed conversation because it merely postpones the conversation that wants and needs to take place. Don't linger on the edges. Small confusions are easy to clear up, but they can also lull you into thinking you've addressed the subject in a comprehensive way. Instead, ask yourself, What is the deepest issue in this confusion, that element that has caused less than spectacular results? Speak toward that with as much courage and clarity as you can muster.

WHAT NOW?

We all have such capacity for love and joy, giving and receiving. I want us fed, not starved! I want us plump and happy. I want us to disappear into food and wine and love and gentleness and devotion. (It's okay to leave out the wine if you must.)

Whether you intend to maintain positive results in your relationships or turn things around, considering all of the conversations you need to have could feel a bit daunting, so consider what the American author E. L. Doctorow said about writing: "It's like driving a car at night. You can only see as far as your headlights illuminate, but you can make the whole trip that way, you see."

It's the same with conversations, so I'd like you to simply take the next phase of your relationship, of your life, *one conversation at a time*. There is within each of us an inner, unexploited wealth, which only rises to the surface in the rare conversations allowed us. Perhaps there are very few conversations in between you and what you desire.

The American spiritual teacher Ram Dass said, "We're all just walking each other home." What will we find when we arrive? I hope that we are talking our homes into sweetness.

What
We speak
Becomes the house we live in.

Who will want to sleep in your bed
If the roof leaks
Right above
It?

Look what happens when the tongue
Cannot say to kindness,

"I will be your slave."

The moon
Covers her face with both hands

And can't bear
To look.

—HAFIZ

In closing, my hope is that your life will become consistent with who you really are or wish to become. I'd like you to consult with yourself before all others, not as a last resort. Have you dreamed of writing? Then write something, anything. Carry a pad and pen in your pocket at all times. Have you always wanted to paint? Then paint something, anything. What's stopping you?

Be kind and truthful always. Above all, enrich your relationships today through every conversation you have. We open our mouths, and in a single sentence we can foster true connection and a fierce love that will withstand the test of time and grow stronger over the years. Say something loving to someone. Don't wait another minute.

With fierce affection,
Susan Scott

Appendix

Practices for a Fierce Life

We are always practicing something. The question is:
What are we practicing?
—MARTIAL ARTS SENSEI

The practices below have contributed greatly to my happiness and fulfillment, which by the way, are two entirely distinct things. We can be happy with the stability of a job, yet mourn the things we haven't pursued. We can be delighted with our children, yet unfulfilled by our achievements apart from family life. In earlier chapters, I've pointed you to conversations with yourself and your partner that will lead to both happiness and fulfillment. Here are a few more thoughts.

CHOOSE YOUR FRIENDS CAREFULLY

Choose your friends carefully and gently walk away from those who do not add joy to your life. My women friends are remarkable.

- Laura, a high school friend and artist, the glue that for decades has held together a cohort of former teenagers, who brought me into the fold when I moved to Kansas City at sixteen and has enfolded me with love ever since.

- Jan, my travel companion, and one of the most capable and creative women I know. She has tools and knows how to use them. Last summer I discovered her high in a pine tree near my tree house, sawing off dead limbs and transforming it into a forty-foot bonsai. Who does that! We've walked the Cotswold Way, explored Paris and Provence, danced with Maasai in Kenya.

- Michele, my island buddy, brave and independent. She started Moonshine Farmacy. Her salves, potions, and tinctures made from old-man's beard, nettles, and other natural wonders are beyond curative—and she makes a mean sage-and-grapefruit cocktail. She nurtured her husband through the stages of ALS and eased him to a sweet and meaningful end by essentially walking him to death, at his request. Their story would be a beautiful movie.

- Maggie, the quintessential English rose who lives in a magical cottage in the New Forest, coach to executives worldwide, and mother to Cameron, a beamish boy who has grown into a truly good man. We hiked in Dingle, Ireland, went falconing, spent a day in the Blasket Islands, filled our souls with live music. I fell in love with the singer Gerry O'Beirne and with an Irish dance performed by an impossibly sexy young man. Each evening we binge-watched *The Crown*.

The people we spend time with impact our lives. As you think about your life, what are you and your friends contributing to one another? What do you talk about? What is the tone of your conversations? How do your friendships impact your emotions? Is this what you want for yourself?

A funny thing happens between people when one of you is really asking and really listening, with sentences that don't trail away in midair, eyes that don't glaze over, and silences that don't make you feel lonelier than you'd feel if you were alone—one who isn't constantly interrupting with his or her own agenda or ascribing negative meanings to everything you say.

If you are spending time with someone who gossips, judges, and criticizes, whose life has basically flatlined, ask yourself why. Are you the one who gossips, judges, criticizes, whose life has flatlined? Ask yourself why. You're better than this. Your friends can be better than this too, so do your best to change the dynamic and, if that isn't possible, make new friends.

LISTEN TO MUSIC THAT
EVOKES FEELING

If you have read my previous books, you know that I write while listening to music because it instantly drops me into a mood and puts me in touch with the parts of myself that I require in that moment. So I choose my music carefully. Think of how music takes possession of us truly, madly, deeply. Now imagine a relationship that touches us as powerfully, as primitively, as completely. This is the essence of fierce love.

I wrote *Fierce Conversations* while listening to Kelly Joe Phelps. I love his sound: a cross between Springsteen, Dock Boggs, and someone from somewhere on the banks of the Mississippi. The lyrics are lovely but secondary. It's simply about what this music evokes in me. Unbidden, dropping me into a funky, smooth, and groovy place where I want to pour a glass of red wine, light a fire, and reminisce. I remember evenings with friends, playing our guitars and singing by the Missouri River during my freshman year of college. I can see Kelly Joe Phelps's music with my eyes. He's tapped into an artery somehow. You can't get that just anywhere.

Different gifts, memories, and emotions would be evoked by listening to Yo-Yo Ma playing Bach's cello suites or to Alasdair Fraser's Scottish fiddle or Mark O'Connor's *Appalachia Waltz*. I discovered Barrington Pheloung through the *Inspector Morse* television series. Ennio Morricone because of *The Mission*.

Like most of you, I have created stations on Pandora. I wrote much of this book to my Chanticleer station, which delightfully includes Eric Whitacre, Redbird, The Wailin' Jennys, John Rutter, Hans Zimmer, Bon Iver, and one of the most beautiful pieces of all: "Sing Me to Heaven" by Daniel E. Gawthrop.

Listening to music that you love will allow you to feel what is there for you to feel, even if you previously locked the door to those emotions and wedged a chair under the knob. That's why we need music, seek it, sometimes avoid it. There are some songs I have to turn off. Just can't take it right now.

PUT DOWN YOUR PHONE, PICK UP A BOOK

Don't just read nonfiction. Pick up a classic work of fiction or a new release. Because I often quote fiction in my writing and talks, people ask me what books I've loved. So many! A few I recommend are, in no particular order:

- *Martin Marten* by Brian Doyle
- *The Unlikely Pilgrimage of Harold Fry* by Rachel Joyce
- *A Man Called Ove* by Fredrik Backman
- Chief Inspector Gamache series by Louise Penny
- *All the Light We Cannot See* by Anthony Doerr
- *H Is for Hawk* by Helen Macdonald
- *Angle of Repose* by Wallace Stegner
- *A Reliable Wife* by Robert Goolrick
- *Independence Day* by Richard Ford

If you want to meet someone who has had an extended fierce conversation with herself and offers that marvelously flawed self to any who care, read *Bird by Bird* or *Traveling Mercies* by Anne Lamott. Read *Pilgrim at Tinker Creek* by Annie Dillard. Or read *A Joseph Campbell Companion*. I fantasize about what it would be like to have these authors as neighbors. When there's a good book in the house, why turn on the TV?

Read poetry. Read good poetry, if possible. Sign up for The Writer's Almanac email newsletter. A poem will arrive every day. Don't try to understand them. You'll know they're good when they evoke something for you . . . a memory, a vivid picture, an emotion, an insight, a trembling of tectonic plates. Read David Whyte's poems. Pick up *The Gift: Poems by Hafiz, the Great Sufi Master,* translated by Daniel Ladinsky. Here was a man happy to be in his own skin. You will smile, you will laugh. Out loud.

GET OFF THE PATH

And take walks. There has been much talk of being on the "path." Too many people are forever seeking, never finding. Why not let the *way* itself arrive? I suspect you already know what to do. For me, the way is an ongoing, robust conversation with all that life has to offer. During walks I converse with lavender roses beside the ocean, quicksilver fishes in alpine lakes, windsong, lapping water, the wide, listening sky. I take my lunch amid the blue-eyed grass and nodding campion at the foot of a laurel that has mated with a copper beech, conversing with my own essential nature. Back at home, the conversation continues with friends and family. What matters is how quickly we do what our souls direct.

A Note to the Reader

Dear reader, I would love for you to tell me the story of a conversation you had as a result of reading this book. With your permission, perhaps your story will be shared with others as part of our online Fierce Love course and podcast. The goal is to take a deeper dive so that we can all learn, gather courage, and create love that lasts.

You can reach me at susan@fierceinc.com.

Our course can be found at https://FierceInc.com/Resources /Fierce-Love/.

Acknowledgments

Bucketfuls of gratitude to Daniel Ladinsky, whose translations of Hafiz's poems in *The Gift* are so beautiful. Thank you, Danny, for allowing me to share two of them in this book. And to William Baer for "Letter of Resignation," Robert Francis for "Summons," and the many authors I've quoted in this book. You said it far better than I could.

More bucketfuls to friends who allowed me to tell their stories.

Thanks to Dianna Kokoszka, who invited me to lead the very first Fierce Love session for several hundred Keller Williams people in Austin, Texas, years ago. Their wholehearted response persuaded me that this book had an audience.

Thanks to my editors, Jen Gingerich, Margot Starbuck, and Brigitta Nortker at Thomas Nelson/HarperCollins for making this a better book. I am not always as clear as I'd like to be, and you three helped solve that problem. And oh, the philosophical debates we had! So useful!

Finally, thank you to Raoul Davis and Leticia Gomez with the Ascendant Group for agenting this book and getting the word out, and to Ed Beltran, Paul Stabile, Luis Gonzales, and my supportive fierce tribe for excusing me from my regular responsibilities so I could focus on writing and developing our online Fierce Love course: FierceInc.com/Resources/ Fierce-Love/.

Oh, and I should thank the men in my life with whom I found a thousand wrong ways to have challenging conversations until we finally got it right. Whew! And also my family: it isn't always easy living with someone who doesn't tiptoe around issues. On the other hand, I'd like to believe I've contributed to my granddaughters' confidence in navigating their relationships. They're pretty spectacular, if I do say so myself.

Every kindness,
Susan Scott
July 2021

Notes

Introduction

xvi "Samuel thought": Nathan Hill, *The Nix* (New York: Knopf Doubleday, 2016), 79.

xvii "The thing about old girlfriends": Anne Tyler, *Redhead by the Side of the Road* (New York: Vintage Books, 2020), 38.

xix "A Night Full of Talking": Coleman Barks, trans., "A Night Full of Talking," in *The Illuminated Rumi* (New York: Broadway, 1997), 18.

xx "The great thing": Ernest Hemingway, *Death in the Afternoon* (1932; repr., New York: Scribner Classics, 2002), 218.

Chapter 1: The Conversation Is the Relationship

6 "The word *conversation*": *Merriam-Webster.com Dictionary*, s.v. "conversation," accessed June 23, 2021, https://www.merriam-webster.com/dictionary /conversation.

7 "I always thought": Kristin Hannah, *The Nightingale* (New York: St. Martin's Press, 2015), 4.

8 "I am myself": "James Taylor Quotes: 'I Am Myself for a Living,'" BrainyQuote, accessed June 24, 2021, https://www.brainyquote.com/quotes /james_taylor_327925.

Chapter 2: Gradually Then Suddenly

11 "Gradually and then suddenly": Ernest Hemingway, *The Sun Also Rises: The Hemingway Library Edition* (New York: Simon & Schuster, 2016), 109.

12 "At first, the difference": Bella Pollen, *The Summer of the Bear* (New York: Atlantic Monthly Press, 2011), 254.

12 "You know before you know": Elizabeth Berg, *Open House* (New York: Random House, 2000), 3.

14 "It is important": William Stafford, "A Ritual to Read to Each Other," in *The Way It Is: New and Selected Poems* (Minneapolis: Graywolf, 1998).

Chapter 3: All Conversations Are with Myself

18 "Pay no attention": *The Wizard of Oz*, directed by Victor Fleming (Beverly Hills, CA: Metro-Goldwyn-Mayer, 1939), quoted in "Pay No Attention to the Man Behind the Curtain," YouTube video, 0:00:11, published by MediaMixTV, June 10, 2016, https://www.youtube.com/watch?v=ivRKfwmgrHY.

18 "We are all tattooed": John T. Morse Jr., *Life and Letters of O. W. Holmes*, 2 vols. (New York: Houghton, Mifflin and Company, 1896), 1:282.

Chapter 4: Crossing the Bold Line

25 "If the boy and girl": "George Lucas Quotes," QuoteFancy, accessed July 15, 2021, https://quotefancy.com/george-lucas-quotes.

25 "I can't live": Badfinger, "Without You," written by Pete Ham and Tom Evans, produced by Geoff Emerick, recorded at Abbey Road Studios, London, July 15 and 29, 1970, track 6 on LP side 1 of *No Dice*, Apple Records, 1970.

25 "the killer song": "Without You (Badfinger song)," Wikipedia, last updated June 13, 2021, https://en.wikipedia.org/wiki/Without_You_(Badfinger _song), quoting Paul McCartney, *VHI Behind the Music*, season 1, episode 107, "1970: Behind the Music," aired April 30, 2000.

26 "In real love": Margaret Anderson, quoted in Stephen Spender, "European Places, People and Events," *New York Times Book Review*, November 18, 1979, 1, https://www.nytimes.com/1979/11/18/archives/european-places-people -and-events-flanner.html.

26 "debonair French musical-comedy star": *Encyclopedia Britannica Online*, s.v. "Maurice Chevalier," last modified January 1, 2021, https://www.britannica .com/biography/Maurice-Chevalier.

26 "Many a man": "Maurice Chevalier Quotes," Quoteland, accessed June 25, 2021, http://www.quoteland.com/author/Maurice-Chevalier-Quotes /3711/.

29 "They could fall in love": Liane Moriarty, *The Husband's Secret* (New York: Berkley Books, 2013), 434–35.

30 "It wasn't that": C. J. Tudor, *The Other People* (New York: Ballantine Books, 2020), 123.

32 "Loving someone": Fredrik Backman, *A Man Called Ove* (New York: Washington Square Press, 2014), 305–6.

Chapter 5: What Isn't *Fierce Love*?

37 "When someone shows you": "Maya Angelou Quotes: When Someone Shows You Who They Are . . . ," BrainyQuote, accessed June 25, 2021, https://www.brainyquote.com/quotes/maya_angelou_383371.

38 "Perhaps you don't": Alison Lurie, *Foreign Affairs* (New York: Random House, 2013), 172–75.

38 "What we do not make conscious": "Quote by Carl Jung: What We Do Not Make Conscious Emerges Later . . . ," Goodreads, accessed June 25, 2021, https://www.goodreads.com/quotes/193530-what-we-do-not-make -conscious-emerges-later-as-fate.

39 "When all else fails": Conan O'Brien, "Conan Addresses the Harvard Class of 2000," streaming video, 21:47, Team Coco, May 30, 2000, https:// teamcoco.com/video/conan-harvard-commencement-speech-2000.

Part 2: The Five Myths That Mislead and Derail Us

45 "If you can't say something": Jean Vanden Heuvel, "The Sharpest Wit in Washington," *Saturday Evening Post*, December 4, 1965, 32.

45 "Perhaps I took": Rachel Joyce, *The Love Song of Miss Queenie Hennessy* (New York: Random House, 2015), 24.

46 "eighty-eight officially recognized constellations": Vicky Stein, "Constellations of the Western Zodiac," Space.com, May 26, 2021, space.com /15722-constellations.html.

46 "The reasonable man": George Bernard Shaw, "Maxims for Revolutionists," in *Man and Superman* (Cambridge, MA: Harvard University Press, 1903), 238.

46 "I believe that": André Gide, *The Journals of André Gide*, trans. and ed. Justin O'Brien, vol. 3, *1928–1939* (London: Secker & Warburg, 1949), 51.

Chapter 6: Myth 1: You Complete Me

52 "How we spend our days": Annie Dillard, *The Writing Life* (1989; repr., New York: Harper Perennial, 2013), 32.

53 "It is better": "André Gide Quote: 'It Is Better to Fail . . . ,'" QuoteFancy,

accessed June 26, 2021, https://quotefancy.com/quote/1011619/Andr-Gide
-It-is-better-to-fail-at-your-own-life-than-to-succeed-at-someone-else-s.

Chapter 7: Myth 2: True Love Is Unconditional

56   "Well, according to Wikipedia": Wikipedia, s.v. *The Giving Tree*," last
updated June 4, 2021, https://en.wikipedia.org/wiki/The_Giving_Tree.

57   "Bob Newhart—Stop It": Bob Newhart, skit on *MADtv*, "Bob Newhart—
Stop It," YouTube video, 6:20, published by Josh Huynh, September 2, 2010,
https://www.youtube.com/watch?v=Ow0lr63y4Mw.

Chapter 8: Myth 3: You Must Fulfill My List

62   "People love each other": Nathan Hill, *The Nix* (New York: Knopf Doubleday,
2016), 99.

63   "affairs are often accepted in France": Richard Wike, "French More
Accepting of Infidelity than People in Other Countries," Pew Research
Center, January 14, 2014, https://www.pewresearch.org/fact-tank/2014/01/14
/french-more-accepting-of-infidelity-than-people-in-other-countries/.

63   "American women expect": W. Somerset Maugham, *The Razor's Edge*
(New York: Doubleday, Doran, 1944), 177.

63   "Keep me from going": Robert Francis, "Summons" from *Collected Poems:
1936-1976* (Amherst: University of Massachusetts Press, 1976), 149.

Chapter 9: Myth 4: If You Loved Me, You'd Know

65   "If you understood everything": Miles Davis, quoted in Victor Svorinich,
Listen to This: Miles Davis and Bitches Brew (Jackson: University Press of
Mississippi, 2015), 158.

66   "She wanted to say": Ford Madox Ford, *Parade's End* (1924; repr., New
York: Wordsworth Classics, 2013), 592.

67   "The idiot's warehouse": Hafiz, "The Idiot's Warehouse," from *The Gift:
Poems by Hafiz, the Great Sufi Master*, trans. Daniel Ladinsky (New York:
Penguin Compass, 1999), 218.

Chapter 11: Conversation 1: Do I Want This Relationship?

84   "I would have girls": Maureen Fitzgerald, *Religion and Feminism in Elizabeth
Cady Stanton's Life and Thought* (Madison: University of Wisconsin, 1985), 71.

86   "How we spend our days": Annie Dillard, *The Writing Life* (1989; repr.,
New York: Harper Perennial, 2013), 32.

Chapter 12: Conversation 2: Clarifying Conditions—Yours, Mine, Ours

91 "At one point Barbara": *The War of the Roses*, directed by Danny DeVito, starring Michael Douglas and Kathleen Turner (Los Angeles: 20th Century Fox, 1989).

93 "Woe-is-me": Maureen Dowd, "Opinion: A Storyteller Loses the Story Line," *New York Times*, June 1, 2010, https://www.nytimes.com/2010/06/02 /opinion/02dowd.html.

Chapter 13: Conversation 3: How Are We Really?

99 "44 percent of marriages": "Provisional Number and Rate of Marriages and Divorces: United States, 2000–2019," Centers for Disease Control and Prevention, accessed July 23, 2021, https://www.cdc.gov/nchs/data/dvs /national-marriage-divorce-rates-00-19.pdf.

99 "average duration of a first marriage": Rose M. Kreider, "Current Population Report: Number, Timing, and Duration of Marriages and Divorces: 2001," Household Economic Studies Publication Series, US Census Bureau, February 2005, https://www.census.gov/prod/2005pubs/p70-97.pdf.

99 "divorce rate of 87 percent": Dominic Nguyen, "Divorce Rate by Country: The World's 10 Most and Least Divorced Nations," Unified Lawyers, updated September 29, 2017, https://www.unifiedlawyers.com.au/blog /global-divorce-rates-statistics/.

99 "fail to bring coffee": "10 Bizarre Divorce Laws," Weinberger Divorce & Family Law Group, April 12, 2012, https://www.weinbergerlawgroup.com /blog/divorce-family-law/10-bizarre-divorce-laws/.

100 "mutually antagonistic things": *Merriam-Webster.com Dictionary*, s.v. "incompatability," accessed June 24, 2021, https://www.merriam-webster .com/dictionary/incompatibility.

100 "no two people": Elizabeth S. Coyle, "Can I File for Divorce on the Grounds of Incompatibility?," *Divorce Magazine*, updated April 26, 2019, https://www .divorcemag.com/articles/is-incompatibility-grounds-for-divorce.

100 "continual compromise": Alex Lickerman, "The Real Reason Couples Decide They're Incompatible," *Psychology Today*, February 3, 2013, https:// www.psychologytoday.com/us/blog/happiness-in-world/201302/the-real -reason-couples-decide-theyre-incompatible.

100 "recent study in Australia": Ilene Wolcott and Jody Hughes, "Toward Understanding the Reasons for Divorce" (working paper, Australian Institute

of Family Studies, Melbourne, June 1999), https://aifs.gov.au/sites/default
/files/publication-documents/WP20.pdf.

100 "31 percent of divorces": "Women More Likely than Men to Initiate
Divorces, but Not Non-Marital Breakups," American Sociological Association,
August 22, 2015, https://www.asanet.org/press-center/press-releases/women
-more-likely-men-initiate-divorces-not-non-marital-breakups.

101 "People change": "Lillian Hellman Quotes: People Change . . . ," BrainyQuote,
accessed June 25, 2021, https://www.brainyquote.com/quotes/lillian
_hellman_105276.

102 "mokita": Nathaniel Scharping, "Do We Need a Word for Everything?,"
Discover Magazine, April 4, 2017, https://www.discovermagazine.com/mind
/do-we-need-a-word-for-everything.

105 "It is also our tradition": Elizabeth Berg, *Tapestry of Fortunes* (New York:
Random House, 2013), 192.

107 "John Gottman": Michael Fulwiler, "Managing Conflict: Solvable vs.
Perpetual Problems," Gottman Institute, July 2, 2012, https://www.gottman
.com/blog/managing-conflict-solvable-vs-perpetual-problems/.

Chapter 14: Conversation 4: Getting Past "Honey, I'm Home"

112 "If you were a bird": Ron Koertge, "Admission Requirements of U.S. and
Canadian Dental Schools," from *Making Love to Roget's Wife: Poems New and
Selected* (Fayetteville: University of Arkansas Press, 1997), 7.

115 "Daniel Kahneman": Deborah Smith, "Psychologist Wins Nobel Prize,"
Monitor on Psychology 33, no. 11 (December 2002): 22, https://www.apa.org
/monitor/dec02/nobel.html.

117 "If I had an hour": "I Would Spend 55 Minutes Defining the Problem and
Then Five Minutes Solving It," Quote Investigator, May 22, 2014, https://
quoteinvestigator.com/2014/05/22/solve/.

Chapter 15: Conversation 5: Let Me Count the Ways

126 "Ken Blanchard's book": Kenneth Blanchard and Spencer Johnson, *The
One Minute Manager* (New York: Berkley Books, 1983).

Chapter 16: Conversation 6: It's Not You, It's Me

131 "*Love Story*": Erich Segal, *Love Story* (1970; repr., New York:
HarperPerennial, 2020), 131.

131 "Barbra Streisand's character": *What's Up, Doc?*, directed by Peter
Bogdanovich (Burbank, CA: Warner Brothers, 1972).

133 "Before speaking": Louise Penny, *A Better Man* (New York: Minotaur Books, 2019), 184.

134 "Life becomes easier": "Quote by Robert Brault," Goodreads, accessed June 29, 2021, https://www.goodreads.com/quotes/857668-life-becomes -easier-when-you-learn-to-accept-an-apology.

Chapter 17: Conversation 7: It's Not Me, It's You

140 "This is not a conversation": Jessie Burton, *The Minaturist* (New York: Ecco, 2014), 121.

143 "Wherever we are in the world": Elizabeth Berg, *Tapestry of Fortunes* (New York: Random House, 2013), 9.

Chapter 18: Conversation 8: I Love You, but I Don't Love Our Life Together

158 "It was more an argument": Fredrik Backman, *A Man Called Ove* (New York: Washington Square Press, 2014), 81.

160 "a zoo of lusts": C. S. Lewis, *Surprised by Joy: The Shape of My Early Life* (1955; repr., New York: HarperOne, 2017), 118.

171 "You've got to learn": Nina Simone, vocalist, "You've Got to Learn," written by Charles Aznavour and Marcel Stellman, track 11 on *I Put a Spell on You*, Philips Records, 1965.

171 "screw your courage": William Shakespeare, *Macbeth*, 1.7.59–61.

Chapter 19: Love After Love

177 "One might argue": Elizabeth George, *A Banquet of Consequences* (2015; repr., New York: Penguin Books, 2021), 105–6.

178 "Letter of Resignation": William Baer, "Letter of Resignation," in *"Bocage" and Other Sonnets* (Huntsville: Texas Review Press, 2008), 31.

179 "Sometimes I wonder": "Quote by Katharine Hepburn: 'Sometimes I Wonder . . . ,'" Goodreads, accessed June 30, 2021, https://www.goodreads.com /quotes/21624-sometimes-i-wonder-if-men-and-women-really-suit-each.

Conclusion: Putting Fierce Love to Work

187 "Human connectivity": Susan Scott, *Fierce Conversations: Achieving Success at Work & in Life, One Conversation at a Time*, rev. ed. (New York: New American Library, 2004), 8–9.

190 "It's like driving": George Plimpton, "E. L. Doctorow: The Art of Fiction No. 94," *Paris Review*, no. 101 (Winter 1986), https://www.theparisreview .org/interviews/2718/the-art-of-fiction-no-94-e-l-doctorow.

190 "We're all just walking": Ram Dass and Mirabai Bush, "Walking Each Other Home: Conversations on Loving and Dying," Ram Dass: Love Serve Remember Foundation, accessed June 23, 2021, https://www.ramdass.org /walking-each-other-home/.

190 "What / We speak": Hafiz, "Covers Her Face with Both Hands," from *The Gift: Poems by Hafiz, the Great Sufi Master*, trans. Daniel Ladinsky (New York: Penguin Compass, 1999), 281.

Appendix: Practices for a Fierce Life

196 "Writer's Almanac email newsletter": You can sign up for the newsletter on Garrison Keillor's website, https://www.garrisonkeillor.com/.

About the Author

Susan Scott is a *New York Times* bestselling author and leadership development architect who for two decades has enabled top executives worldwide to engage in vibrant dialogue with one another, with their employees, and with their customers. She pioneered the process of fierce conversations that has touched the lives of millions of people, and now she's freshly applying these ideas to our romantic relationships. Susan lives in Medina, Washington.

Accompanying journal available now!